Ancient African Empires

An Enthralling Guide to the Major Kingdoms and Civilizations of Africa

© Copyright 2024 - All rights reserved.

The content contained within this book may not be reproduced, duplicated, or transmitted without direct written permission from the author or the publisher.

Under no circumstances will any blame or legal responsibility be held against the publisher, or author, for any damages, reparation, or monetary loss due to the information contained within this book, either directly or indirectly.

Legal Notice:

This book is copyright protected. It is only for personal use. You cannot amend, distribute, sell, use, quote, or paraphrase any part, or the content within this book, without the consent of the author or publisher.

Disclaimer Notice:

Please note the information contained within this document is for educational and entertainment purposes only. All effort has been executed to present accurate, up-to-date, reliable, and complete information. No warranties of any kind are declared or implied. Readers acknowledge that the author is not engaging in the rendering of legal, financial, medical, or professional advice. The content within this book has been derived from various sources. Please consult a licensed professional before attempting any techniques outlined in this book.

By reading this document, the reader agrees that under no circumstances is the author responsible for any losses, direct or indirect, that are incurred as a result of the use of the information contained within this document, including, but not limited to, errors, omissions, or inaccuracies.

Free limited time bonus

Stop for a moment. We have a free bonus set up for you. The problem is this: we forget 90% of everything that we read after 7 days. Crazy fact, right? Here's the solution: we've created a printable, 1-page pdf summary for this book that you're reading now. All you have to do to get your free pdf summary is to go to the following website: https://livetolearn.lpages.co/enthrallinghistory/

Or, Scan the QR code!

Once you do, it will be intuitive. Enjoy, and thank you!

Table of Contents

INTRODUCTION 1
PART 1: HUMBLE BEGINNINGS..3
    CHAPTER 1: THE STONE AGE AND THE FIRST CIVILIZATIONS 4
    CHAPTER 2: THE AGE OF GREAT METALS: COPPER, BRONZE,
    AND IRON AGES..12
PART 2: KINGDOMS AND CIVILIZATIONS..19
    CHAPTER 3: KUSH 20
    CHAPTER 4: AKSUM 27
    CHAPTER 5: PUNT: A FARAWAY LAND?..37
PART 3: THE GREAT EMPIRES AND THEIR LEGACIES 45
    CHAPTER 6: ANCIENT EGYPT 46
    CHAPTER 7: KERMA 74
    CHAPTER 8: ANCIENT CARTHAGE 79
    CHAPTER 9: EMPIRE OF GHANA 93
    CHAPTER 10: SLAVERY IN ANCIENT AFRICA 100
CONCLUSION..106
HERE'S ANOTHER BOOK BY ENTHRALLING HISTORY THAT
YOU MIGHT LIKE...114
FREE LIMITED TIME BONUS..115
BIBLIOGRAPHY 116

Introduction

Welcome to the captivating world of ancient African empires. Get ready to embark on a remarkable journey through time to explore the awe-inspiring stories of civilizations that once thrived on the African continent. This book will transport you to the heart of ancient Africa, where powerful empires rose and fell.

The contribution of African empires to world history and civilization is significant, but it remains largely unexplored. This book attempts to change this. We will unravel the enigmatic tales of some of the most illustrious empires in the annals of human civilization, focusing primarily on Egypt, Carthage, and Nubia. We will also investigate the fabled kingdoms of Kush, Aksum, and Punt.

Understanding the legacies of African history provides a profound insight into the roots of human civilization. These empires laid the foundations for cultural, technological, and societal advancements that continue to influence our world today. The diverse array of empires showcased here underscores the incredible diversity and dynamism that has always been a part of Africa.

The book has simplified the complex historical facts and events surrounding these ancient empires into easy-to-understand language. We know how mundane history books can be. They leave the reader feeling lost or confused. Our goal is to make you feel engaged with the past and eager to learn more.

Prepare to be captivated by the grandeur of pyramids, the brilliance of military strategists, the mystique of ancient rituals, and the resilience of civilizations that thrived in a land where history's echoes still resound today.

Part 1: Humble Beginnings

Chapter 1: The Stone Age and the First Civilizations

Africa is called the Cradle of Humankind, as it is believed human life began there. The Stone Age was a time of learning and developing the customs, skills, and political organizations that evolved into sophisticated civilizations. Three distinct eras comprise what we refer to as the Stone Age and the beginning of modern human beings.

<u>The Paleolithic Era</u>

The Paleolithic era is the earliest period in human history. It spans from approximately 2.5 million years ago to around 10,000 BCE in Africa. During this time, human ancestors lived as hunter-gatherers, relying on the land's natural resources to survive. In Africa, the Paleolithic era was marked by the use of stone and rock tools, which were essential for hunting, cutting, and other crucial tasks for survival. These tools were primarily crafted from flint, chert, obsidian, and other locally available stones. Acheulean hand axes, a distinctive type of bifacial tool characterized by their teardrop shape, were commonly used during the Lower Paleolithic (the earliest part of the Paleolithic era). These hand axes were versatile tools used for cutting, chopping, and butchering.

Different views of an Acheulean hand ax.
Muséum de Toulouse, CC BY-SA 4.0 <https://creativecommons.org/licenses/by-sa/4.0>, via Wikimedia Commons;
https://commons.wikimedia.org/wiki/File:Biface_Cintegabelle_MHNT_PRE_2009.0.201.1_V2.jpg

The Middle Paleolithic saw the emergence of more sophisticated tools, such as the Levallois technique, which allowed for the production of specialized flakes and blades. These innovations indicate an increased level of cognitive and technical skills among Paleolithic populations.

Paleolithic humans in Africa were primarily nomadic hunter-gatherers. They relied on hunting animals like antelope, buffalo, and wild boar, as well as gathering edible plants, fruits, and nuts. The discovery of fossilized animal bones with cut marks and stone tools at sites like Olduvai Gorge in Tanzania provides strong evidence of early hunting and butchering practices during the Paleolithic era.[1]

Mastery of fire was a significant milestone during the Paleolithic era. The ability to control and use fire provided people with warmth, protection, and the means to cook food, which profoundly impacted diet and survival. Archaeological sites like Wonderwerk Cave in South Africa have yielded evidence of early hearths and the use of fire, dating back over a million years.

Saharan Rock Art

Throughout the Paleolithic era, culture and technology gradually evolved. This evolution is marked by the development of new tool types, increased social complexity, and potential regional variations. While less

---

[1] Kessing, F. M. (2024, January 9). Stone Age-African Tools, Artifacts, Culture. Retrieved from Britannca.com: https://www.britannica.com/event/Stone-Age/Africa.

prevalent than in later periods, some evidence of artistic expression exists from the Paleolithic era in Africa. This includes rock art, engravings, and sculptures.

One of Africa's most intriguing aspects of the Paleolithic era is Saharan rock art. These ancient artworks provide a window into the lives and beliefs of early Africans. Found in various regions of the Sahara Desert, these rock paintings and engravings depict scenes of daily life, animals, and spiritual or ritualistic motifs. They offer valuable insights into ancient African communities' artistic and cultural expressions. The Blombos Cave in South Africa contains engraved pieces of ochre, suggesting early symbols or creative behavior.[2]

Wall art found in a cave in Chad.
David Stanley from Nanaimo, Canada, CC BY 2.0
<https://creativecommons.org/licenses/by/2.0>, *via Wikimedia Commons;*
https://commons.wikimedia.org/wiki/File:Prehistoric_Rock_Paintings_at_Manda_Gu%C3%9Ii_Cave_in_the_Ennedi_Mountains_-_northeastern_Chad_2015.jpg

As the climate and environment in Africa fluctuated over the Paleolithic era, humans had to adapt to changing conditions. This likely played a role in shaping their tool-making techniques and resource

---

[2] Museum, T. B. (2024, January 9). Rock art and the origins of art in Africa. Retrieved from Khanacademy.org: https://www.khanacademy.org/humanities/ap-art-history/global-prehistory-ap/paleolithic-mesolithic-neolithic-apah/a/apollo-11-stones.

exploitation strategies. During periods of climatic change, when large parts of Africa became drier, Paleolithic populations adapted by moving to more favorable regions and adjusting their subsistence strategies accordingly.[3]

The Mesolithic Era

The Mesolithic era in Africa, also known as the Middle Stone Age, was a transitional period that followed the Paleolithic era and preceded the Neolithic era. This era spanned from around 10,000 to 5000 BCE and witnessed significant changes in human societies and their ways of life. The Mesolithic era marked the shift from nomadic hunter-gatherer lifestyles to more settled and organized communities, setting the stage for the later emergence of agriculture and the Neolithic Revolution. While hunting and gathering remained important, Mesolithic communities began to establish more permanent camps and were not roaming constantly.

In the Mesolithic period, stone tools became more specialized and refined. While some of the tools continued to be made from stone, there was experimentation with other materials, such as bone and wood, leading to the development of new tool types. The creation of microliths, tiny and highly efficient stone blades, was a notable development. Microliths were used as components for composite tools, such as spears and arrows, indicating an advancement in hunting technology.

Art in the Mesolithic Era

Mesolithic African communities left behind evidence of cultural expression, although it was less elaborate than in later periods. This included the creation of small-scale art, such as carvings and engravings on bones, stone, and shells. The Apollo 11 Cave in Namibia dates to the Mesolithic period and contains some of the earliest known examples of portable art in Africa. These artifacts include engraved pieces of stone with geometric and abstract designs.[4]

---

[3] Smithsonian Institute. (2024, January 3). Climate Effects on Human Evolution. Retrieved from Humanorigons.si.edu: https://humanorigins.si.edu/research/climate-and-human-evolution/climate-effects-human-evolution.

[4] Cerise Myers, E. C. (2024, January 9). 5.2 Mesolithic Art. Retrieved from Libretexts.org: https://human.libretexts.org/Bookshelves/Art/Introduction_to_Art_History_I_%28Myers%29/05%3A_Art_of_the_Stone_Age/5.02%3A_Mesolithic_Art.

Societal Changes

The Mesolithic era in Africa coincided with climatic fluctuations, including the transition from the Last Glacial Maximum to a warmer and more stable climate. As a result, human populations had to adapt to changing environmental conditions. Populations began to adjust to regional environments and resource availability. This period saw a diversification in the types of foods consumed, including a greater reliance on marine resources in coastal regions. Coastal Mesolithic communities in areas like the South African coastline engaged in shellfish gathering and fishing, utilizing both marine and terrestrial resources for their sustenance.

The Mesolithic period witnessed innovations in social organization and technology. While not as complex as the societies of the Neolithic period, there was evidence of increased social cooperation and the development of more sophisticated tools. The emergence of fishing technology, including harpoons and fishnets, suggests a level of coordination and specialization within Mesolithic communities as they adapted to aquatic resources.[5]

Africa witnessed a lot of migration during the Mesolithic era. Major language groups, such as the Niger-Congo, started to be noticed as the Sahara became drier. The Bantu later spread into central, eastern, and southern Africa, displacing indigenous people like the Pygmies.

Societies were formed due to the development of tribal relations. The division of labor based on gender, with the men doing the hunting and fishing and women taking care of plant-based food, was typical.[6] Transition ceremonies from child to adult with established initiation rites happened. These ceremonies and trials passed on the working habits, oral traditions, and sacred knowledge from one generation to the next.[7]

---

[5] Kessing, F. M. (2024, January 9). Stone Age-African Tools, Artifacts, Culture. Retrieved from Britannca.com: https://www.britannica.com/event/Stone-Age/Africa.

[6] It must be noted that the division of labor was not set in stone. Times of need might call for women to aid in hunting or men to pick plants. Different tribal groups would have practiced different traditions as well. However, broadly speaking, men typically hunted while women gathered plants and other materials.

[7] S., A. (2015, December 21). Mesolithic Social Life and Art. Retrieved from Shorthistory.org: https://www.shorthistory.org/prehistory/mesolithic-social-life-and-art/.

The Mesolithic era in Africa represents a crucial phase in human history, bridging the gap between the Paleolithic hunter-gatherer lifestyle and the agricultural revolution of the Neolithic period. It was a time of experimentation, adaptation, and the gradual development of technologies and social structures that paved the way for profound changes.

The Neolithic Era

The Neolithic era, often referred to as the Late Stone Age, was a transformative period in Africa that followed the Mesolithic era. The Neolithic period marked a significant shift in human societies, characterized by the widespread adoption of agriculture, animal domestication, and more settled, agricultural-based communities. The Neolithic era in Africa ranged from around 5000 to 2000 BCE, depending on the region.

Food Production

The most defining feature of the Neolithic era was the development of agriculture. African societies began cultivating crops and farming animals, providing a more reliable and abundant food supply. In the Nile Valley of Egypt, the cultivation of wheat and barley was practiced as early as 5000 BCE, transforming the region into a breadbasket and enabling population growth.

Consistent with the move to farming, the Neolithic period saw the domestication of animals for various purposes, including providing meat, milk, wool, and labor. This marked a crucial step in human history, leading to more complex and diversified economies. In North Africa, the domestication of cattle and sheep became prominent. The Saharan region saw the emergence of pastoral societies, which relied on herding domesticated animals for sustenance.

Settling Down

Neolithic communities established more permanent settlements, transitioning from the semi-nomadic lifestyle of their Mesolithic ancestors. These communities often built more substantial structures and engaged in rudimentary urban planning. The Nabta Playa archaeological site in the Nubian Desert reveals evidence of complex stone structures similar to Stonehenge, potentially serving as markers for astronomical events. These structures suggest a level of social organization and architectural planning.[8]

As African populations settled into permanent communities and worked to generate surplus food, Neolithic societies had the opportunity to engage in specialized crafts and develop more sophisticated tools and technologies. The use of pottery became widespread during this period. Neolithic Africans created pottery vessels for storage, cooking, and ceremonial purposes. Pottery enabled more efficient food processing and storage.[9]

Social Hierarchy and Society

As populations grew and communities became more settled, social hierarchies and organizational structures emerged. Leadership roles and divisions of labor became more defined. Small villages or clan settlements eventually evolved into city-states. Agriculture was the main driver of complex social structures in the Neolithic era.

Examples of substantial Neolithic settlements were found in Egypt's Western Desert. Sheikh el-Obeiyid has twenty-five circular and oval huts. Another significant archaeological find is Site 270 at Dakhla Oasis. Archaeologists uncovered two hundred circular and rectangular stone huts grouped in clusters that might have been social groups. These suggest evidence of community planning. Large communal buildings (some as long as twelve meters) might have served as centers of authority or for rituals.[10]

The Neolithic era in Africa laid the foundations for more complex and enduring societies on the continent. The shift from hunting and gathering to agriculture and animal husbandry was a revolutionary leap that led to population growth, technological innovations, and the rise of early civilizations.

---

[8] Smith, P. (2015, September 16). Nabta Playa: The Oldest Man-Made Structure in the World. Retrieved from Historic Cornwell: https://www.historic-cornwall.org.uk/nabta-playa-the-oldest-man-made-structure-in-the-world/.

[9] Huysecom, E. (2024, January 9). Arguments for an Early Neolithic in Sub-Saharan Africa. Retrieved from Ounjougou.org: https://www.ounjougou.org/en/projects/mali/archaeology/arguments-for-an-early-neolithic-in-sub-saharan-africa/.

[10] Ancient Egypt Magazine. (2023, February 6). Neolithic Settlements of the Western Desert: Proto-villages of Stone Age Egypt. Retrieved from the-past.com: https://the-past.com/feature/neolithic-settlements-of-the-western-desert-proto-villages-of-stone-age-egypt/.

In Summary

The Paleolithic, Mesolithic, and Neolithic periods are the underpinnings of early African civilizations. When we look at the Stone Age, from its use of stone tools that gradually developed into more complex tools to the Saharan rock art that communicates the lives and aspirations of early folk to the transition from nomadic hunter-gatherer societies to settled agricultural communities, we can see the first steps in the evolution of later cultures.

These pivotal developments laid the groundwork for the rise of the first great African civilizations, setting the stage for a rich and enduring history.

Chapter 2: The Age of Great Metals: Copper, Bronze, and Iron Ages

In this chapter, we will delve into three major eras that shaped Africa's ancient past: the Copper Age, the Bronze Age, and the Iron Age. Each era represents a significant leap forward in the continent's cultural, economic, and technological landscape. To provide a comprehensive understanding, we will explore the key developments and innovations in each period and offer a timeline to illustrate the progression of events.

<u>The Copper Age in Africa (c. 4000 BCE-c. 2500 BCE)</u>

One of the most significant developments of the Copper Age was the discovery and utilization of copper for various purposes. Early African societies learned to extract copper ore from mines and develop smelting techniques to separate copper from its ore. This marked the inception of metallurgy in Africa.

While the exact timeline and specific details of the earliest copper metallurgy in Africa vary by region, it is clear that by around 4000 BCE, several African societies were already experimenting with copper working, marking the beginning of the Copper Age in the continent.

Evidence of early copper metallurgy comes from sites like Buhen in Egypt and various locations in the Agadez Region of Niger. These sites contain copper artifacts and remnants of copper mining and smelting activities. The copper used during this period was often relatively pure, known as native copper, which could be found in nugget form in certain geological formations.

Technological Advancements

Copper metallurgy brought about several significant technological advancements that had far-reaching impacts. For instance, early African metallurgists developed methods for heating copper ore to separate the metal from impurities, laying the groundwork for more sophisticated metallurgical processes in later ages.

Copper Age societies also began using copper to create a wide range of tools and weapons. Copper's malleability allowed for the production of more durable and practical tools than those made from stone, bone, or wood. Copper tools included knives, axes, chisels, and spearheads, which significantly improved agricultural practices, construction, and hunting.

As copper metallurgy advanced, specialized artisans who were skilled in working with copper emerged. These artisans played a pivotal role in producing intricate copper artifacts, such as jewelry and ornaments. This specialization contributed to developing a distinct artisan class within African societies.

Settled Communities

Copper tools allowed for more efficient farming practices, resulting in increased food production and population growth. This shift marked the beginning of more complex social structures and sedentary lifestyles.

Copper objects were used in rituals and ceremonies. Copper was used for sculptures in Africa, as evidenced by a life-sized statue of Pharoah Pepi I, who ruled in the Sixth Dynasty (c. 2325-2150 BCE).

Head of Pepi I's life-sized statue.
Jon Bodsworth, Copyrighted free use, via Wikimedia Commons;
https://commons.wikimedia.org/wiki/File:PepiI-CopperStatue-Cropped.png

Overall, the Copper Age in ancient Africa was a pivotal phase in the continent's history, marked by the emergence of metallurgy, technological innovation, economic growth through trade and interaction, and the beginnings of settled societies. These developments laid the foundation for future advancements in metalworking and the evolution of African civilizations.

<u>Timeline of Key Events in the Copper Age</u>
- 4000 BCE: Earliest evidence of copper working.
- 3500 BCE: Expansion of copper usage across different regions.
- 2500 BCE: Transition to the Bronze Age.

The Bronze Age in Africa (c. 2500 BCE-c. 1000 BCE)

The Bronze Age in ancient Africa, spanning from approximately 2500 to 1000 BCE, saw African societies make the transition from using primarily copper to using the alloy known as bronze, which is composed of copper and tin.

African societies discovered the art of alloying copper with tin, resulting in the creation of bronze. This alloy, characterized by its strength and durability, represented a significant advancement in metallurgical technology.

The adoption of bronze tools revolutionized agriculture during the Bronze Age. Bronze plows and hoes improved soil cultivation, making farming more efficient. Enhanced agricultural productivity led to surpluses, population growth, and the development of larger, more intricate societies. Introducing bronze for weaponry significantly improved defense capabilities and influenced military strategies. Bronze swords, spears, and armor became standard equipment, altering the dynamics of conflicts and power in the region.

Importance of Trade

Tin is a necessary ingredient for making bronze, and although there are tin deposits in central and southern Africa, there is no conclusive evidence there was an inner-African trade in tin during the Bronze Age. Egypt had tin reserves in the Eastern Desert, but these might only have been mined after 2000 BCE. Mesopotamia had tin deposits and might have shipped the metal as far west as Crete. Oxhide ingots, metal slabs that made it easier to transport copper or tin, might have been exported to Egypt in exchange for goods like ostrich egg shells. By way of Egypt, Africa became part of the eastern Mediterranean trade network, and trade stimulated the expansion of urban centers.[11]

Society and Art

The Bronze Age witnessed the emergence of more complex societies across the African continent. These urban hubs served as focal points for a myriad of advancements. Monumental architecture, such as the Karnak Temple Complex, demonstrated the power and affluence of

---

[11] Robert Maddin, T. S. (1977). Tin in the Ancient Near East: Old Questions and New Finds. Retrieved from Penn Museum: https://www.penn.museum/sites/expedition/tin-in-the-ancient-near-east/.

kingdoms. Bronze transcended its utilitarian role and played a vital part in artistic expression and architectural innovation.[12]

Egypt had its glory years during the Bronze Age. Urban centers, such as Thebes, showcased the might of this nation, and art was created on a grand scale. Tombs give us a glimpse into the grandeur of the pharaohs. Egyptian gods were a significant artistic inspiration, although Egyptian art also often depicted pharaohs and animals. An essential artifact from the Egyptian Bronze Age is the Narmer Palette with its semi-nude figures.

The cultural and artistic flowering during the Bronze Age continues to inspire and influence Africa's history and cultural heritage. It stands as a testament to the adaptability and ingenuity of ancient African societies in shaping the course of their history and civilization.

Timeline of Key Events in the Bronze Age
- 2500 BCE: Advent of bronze metallurgy.
- 1800 BCE: Flourishing bronze trade networks.
- 1000 BCE: Transition to the Iron Age.

The Iron Age in Africa (c. 1000 BCE–c. 500 CE)

During the Iron Age, African societies experienced a profound transformation as they transitioned from the use of copper and bronze to iron. Iron was once thought to have originated in Egypt, but new evidence suggests that ironworking technology independently developed and predated Egypt in what is now Chad, the Central African Republic, and South Sudan and spread west along the Niger River to the Nok culture of West Africa. Bantu migrations helped spread the technology.[13]

One of the defining features of the Iron Age in Africa was the mastery of iron metallurgy. Iron ore, abundant in western and southern Africa, became the primary source for crafting tools, weapons, and various other essential items.

---

[12] College Sidekick.com. (2024, January 13). The Bronze Age. Retrieved from Collegesidekick.com: https://www.collegesidekick.com/study-guides/boundless-arthistory/the-bronze-age.

[13] Openstax.org. (2024, January 13). 9.2 The Emergence of Farming and the Bantu Migrations. Retrieved from Openstax.org: https://openstax.org/books/world-history-volume-1/pages/9-2-the-emergence-of-farming-and-the-bantu-migrations.

Agriculture

The availability of iron tools revolutionized agriculture across Africa. Iron plows and hoes replaced their less durable predecessors, allowing farmers to till the soil even more efficiently than before. They could cultivate more significant areas of land, which boosted crop yields. This agricultural revolution profoundly impacted food production, leading to surpluses, population growth, and the emergence of more complex societies.

Military Advances

The durability and effectiveness of iron in weaponry transformed the nature of warfare in Africa. Iron swords, spears, and shields became standard equipment for armies, leading to more advanced military strategies and tactics. The ability to produce iron weapons in more significant quantities and with higher quality influenced the power dynamics of the time, often determining the rise and fall of kingdoms and empires.

Rise of Urban Centers and Trade

The Iron Age witnessed the growth of urban centers and the formation of complex societies. These urban hubs served as focal points for trade, administration, and cultural exchange. Advanced architectural structures characterized their development, including city walls, palaces, and ceremonial centers. This transformation led to the establishment of political hierarchies and state structures, resulting in the rise of influential African kingdoms and empires.

The increased production of iron tools, as well as agricultural surpluses, facilitated the growth of extensive trade networks. African goods, including iron tools, precious metals, and agricultural products, were traded within the continent and with neighboring regions. West Africa significantly benefited from the mastery of iron metallurgy. Iron gave rise to the Kingdom of Ife and other important Nigerian kingdoms.[14]

Art during the Iron Age

Ironwork went beyond useful tools; it played a significant role in creative expression and architectural innovation. Iron artifacts,

---

[14] Ross, E. G. (2002, October). The Age of Iron in West Africa. Retrieved from Metmuseum.org: https://www.metmuseum.org/toah/hd/iron/hd_iron.htm.

sculptures, and decorative elements adorned religious and ceremonial spaces, reflecting the diversity of artistic traditions and beliefs across various African societies.

Iron was used in West Africa for jewelry, art, and musical instruments. It had spiritual significance in many African cultures. These artistic creations showcased the richness of cultural expression and served as a testament to the creativity and craftsmanship of the era.

Iron artifacts were often used in religious ceremonies and rituals, as they were believed to possess mystical properties. Evidence of the ritual use of iron furnaces can be found in Tanzania and Rwanda.[15]

The Iron Age's legacy continues to influence Africa's history and cultural heritage. It paved the way for subsequent periods of innovation and progress on the continent.

Timeline of Key Events in the Iron Age
- 1000 BCE: Emergence of ironworking.
- 500 BCE: Rise of prominent African kingdoms.
- 500 CE: Transition to medieval African history.

In Summary

The Copper, Bronze, and Iron Ages in Africa represent a remarkable journey of innovation, cultural expression, and societal transformation. These eras not only mark technological milestones but also highlight the resilience and adaptability of African civilizations. Understanding the timelines and key developments in each age allows us to better appreciate these ancient African societies.

---

[15] Academic Accelerator. (2024, January 13). Archaeological Evidence for the Origins and Spread of Iron Production in Africa. Retrieved from Academic-accelerator.com: https://academic-accelerator.com/encyclopedia/iron-metallurgy-in-africa.

Part 2: Kingdoms and Civilizations

Chapter 3: Kush

The Nile River has been the home of people for millennia. The enigmatic Kingdom of Kush was situated along the banks of the river. This ancient civilization, known for its rich history and significant influence, is a captivating subject of study for historians, archaeologists, and scholars. Its relationship with Egypt ebbed and flowed, causing interesting developments that, at one time, led to the conqueror becoming the conquered.

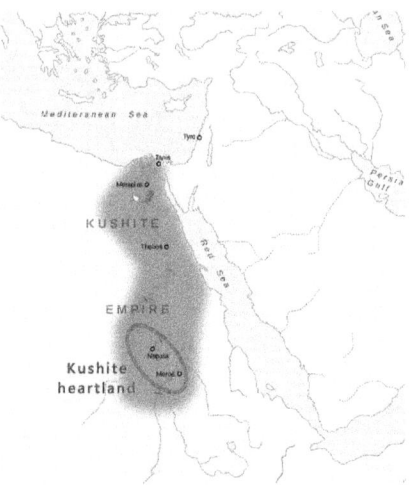

The Kingdom of Kush around 700 BCE.
Original map: Lommes Addition of Kushite heartland; Source: National Geographic 2019, CC BY-SA 4.0 <https://creativecommons.org/licenses/by-sa/4.0>, via Wikimedia Commons; https://commons.wikimedia.org/wiki/File:Kushite_heartland_and_Kushite_Empire_of_the_25th_dynasty_circa_700_BCE.jpg

The Location of Kush

Kush was an ancient African civilization that existed from around 1070 BCE to 350 CE. Its diverse economy played a significant role in the region's trade networks, making it economically crucial to Egypt and other neighboring civilizations.

Also known as Nubia, Kush flourished for millennia, encompassing modern-day Sudan and southern Egypt. Information about this civilization comes from a combination of archaeological discoveries, inscriptions, and references in the records of neighboring ancient civilizations.

Excavations in the Nile Valley have unearthed a wealth of material evidence, including architecture, pottery, jewelry, and burial sites. For instance, the ancient city of Kerma was a pivotal center of the Kush, and extensive archaeological findings there have provided invaluable insights into Kushite culture and history. The oldest known reference to Kush in ancient Egyptian texts dates back to around 2300 BCE. The Egyptians referred to Kush as "Kas" or "Kas-ti," and these references talked about the land south of Egypt and the interactions between the two regions.

The Economy of Kush

Kush was not an impoverished backwater. Like its northern neighbor, Egypt, it was a prosperous region that drew much of its wealth from the Nile. Agriculture was the backbone of the Kushite economy. The fertile Nile River valley provided an excellent environment for farming. Kushites cultivated crops like wheat, barley, sorghum, and various vegetables. They also engaged in pastoralism, raising cattle, goats, and sheep. The Nile's annual flooding ensured fertile soil for their agricultural activities.

The Nile supplied more than the water needed to grow crops. It was a major factor in the Kushites' commercial economy. Kush was strategically located along the Nile, making it a crucial trade hub. The Kingdom of Kush served as a bridge between Egypt to the north and sub-Saharan Africa to the south. Kush's geographical position at the crossroads of trade routes between Egypt and the African interior made it a commercial hub of significant importance. Some of the commodities that contributed to its commercial value included gold, ivory, and exotic goods.

Kush was known for its gold deposits, especially in the Nubian Desert and the Red Sea Hills. The Kingdom of Kush was a significant source of gold for Egypt and other Mediterranean civilizations. The Egyptian pharaohs were especially interested in maintaining good relations with Kush so they could enjoy a steady supply of this precious metal.

The Kingdom of Kush controlled the ivory trade, a highly sought-after valuable commodity by neighboring regions. Kush also facilitated the exchange of various exotic goods, such as rare woods, gemstones, and luxury items, which further enhanced its commercial significance.[16]

Kush controlled the upper reaches of the Nile River, which allowed it to regulate and tax trade that passed through its territory. Its control over the Nile also allowed it to impose tolls and tariffs on goods passing along the river.

Kushite Society

Like many ancient societies, Kush had a hierarchical social structure. The ruling class was at the top of the hierarchy, which included the monarchs (kings and queens) and the nobility. Beneath them were priests, administrators, and military leaders. The common people comprised most of the population, including farmers, artisans, and laborers. Since the Kushites engaged in the slave trade, it is likely their society had enslaved people in it as well.

Religion played a significant role in Kushite society. There was no formal Kushite religion, and the people practiced a blend of indigenous African religious beliefs and Egyptian-inspired religious traditions. The emphasis of their religion was for a person to be one with the natural world and live in harmony. They worshiped a pantheon of deities and often incorporated Egyptian gods and goddesses into their religious practices. Sebiumeker, lord of fertility and procreation, was a principal god. Temples and religious monuments, such as the Lion Temple at Naqa, were important centers.

The Kushite society spoke Kushitic, which was likely part of the Nilo-Saharan language family. However, the elite and educated class used a writing system heavily influenced by Egyptian hieroglyphics.[17]

---

[16] Kemezis, K. (2009, November 22). Ancient Kush (2nd Millennium B.C. - 4th Century A.D.). Retrieved from Blackpast.org: https://www.blackpast.org/global-african-history/ancient-kush-2nd-millennium-b-c-4th-century-d/.

[17] Marc. (2022, October 14). The Kush Kingdom: A Major Power in the Ancient World. Retrieved from Ilovelanguages.com: https://www.ilovelanguages.com/the-kush-kingdom-a-major-power-in-the-ancient-world/.

Art and Architecture

Being strategically located at the crossroads of African and Mediterranean trade routes, Kushite society had extensive interactions with neighboring civilizations, including Egypt, the Mediterranean world, and other African societies. These interactions influenced their culture and art.

Kushite society had a rich artistic and cultural heritage. They developed an artistic style, often characterized by narrative wall paintings, egg-shell thin pottery, and bronze statues of deities and monarchs. The Kingdom of Kush is renowned for its distinctive, steep-sided pyramids, which were used as tombs for royalty and nobility. Notable examples exist at Meroë and Jebel Barkal.[18]

The economic ties between Egypt and Kush also led to cultural exchange. Egyptian art, technology, and religious beliefs influenced Kushite culture and vice versa—the exchange of ideas and practices enriched both civilizations.

Governance

The political structure of Kush evolved over the years. The region gradually transitioned from a series of independent city-states to a powerful kingdom. Kush rose on the ashes of an earlier civilization, Kerma, and would be the foundation for its successor state, Meroë. Each had its own rulers and centralized authority and were distinct phases of the development of Kush as a kingdom and a civilization.

Kush c. 1070–300 BCE

After the decline of the Kerma Kingdom (which has its own chapter later in this book), the Kingdom of Kush emerged in the Napata region, near modern-day Karima in Sudan. The Kushite Kingdom adopted elements of Egyptian culture and religion, including the worship of Egyptian deities. The rulers of Napata constructed pyramids similar to those of Egypt, symbolizing their status and influence. The most famous of these is the Pyramid of Taharqa. Kush eventually faced political challenges from the Assyrians and Persians and was succeeded by the Meroitic Kingdom.

---

[18] Kemezis, K. (2009, November 22). Ancient Kush (2nd Millennium B.C. - 4th Century A.D.). Retrieved from Blackpast.org: https://www.blackpast.org/global-african-history/ancient-kush-2nd-millennium-b-c-4th-century-d/.

Meroitic Kingdom (300 BCE-350 CE.)

The Meroitic Kingdom was the most enduring period of Kushite civilization. It was centered in the city of Meroë, located near the modern town of Shendi in Sudan.

One of the most distinctive features of the Meroitic Kingdom was its own script, known as Meroitic writing, which remains only partially deciphered. Meroitic Cursive was used for record-keeping, and Meroitic Hieroglyphs was used for inscriptions on monuments and documents. The Meroitic Kingdom was known for its advanced ironworking industry, producing high-quality iron tools and weapons.

The Meroitic Kingdom declined, possibly due to a combination of factors, including invasions and internal rebellions. The Kingdom of Aksum eventually replaced it in the 4th century CE.

The Egyptian Connection

Kush's geographical location made it a strategic partner for Egypt. The two kingdoms often engaged in diplomacy, alliances, and trade agreements. Egypt relied on Kush for valuable resources and materials, like gold and incense, which were essential for religious and economic purposes. In return, Kush benefited from Egypt's military and political support, helping it maintain its independence and security.

The conquest of Kerma by the Egyptians was a setback, but it did not mean the Kushites would fade into history. They returned to prominence several centuries later. The rise of the Kingdom of Kush around 1070 BCE is often associated with the decline of the New Kingdom of Egypt and the disintegration of Egyptian control over its southern territories.

The New Kingdom of Egypt began to experience internal strife and external threats. Pharaohs became weaker, and Egypt was divided by power struggles and competing rulers. The Twentieth Dynasty of Egypt (c. 1186-1069 BCE) was marked by political instability and the decline of centralized authority, creating a power vacuum that allowed external forces to gain influence.

Egypt faced invasions by various foreign powers during this period. The Libyans' and Sea Peoples' invasions disrupted Egyptian rule and weakened central authority. The Libyans managed to establish themselves in the Nile Delta. Egypt was too busy fighting off attackers in the north to be concerned about what was happening in the south. Kush continued to control important trade routes that connected Egypt with the African interior, which allowed the Kushites to gain wealth and resources and further strengthen their position in the region.

Once Conquered, Now the Conquerors

Kushite rulers extended their influence into Upper Egypt, taking control of key cities and regions. Their presence and authority in Upper Egypt challenged the remnants of Egyptian rule and further established Kushite dominance in the area.

The Kingdom of Kush launched a series of military campaigns in Egypt. These campaigns were led by Kushite rulers who aimed to assert their authority over Egyptian territories. The Kushite rulers formed alliances with local Egyptian leaders who were dissatisfied with the existing political fragmentation. These local leaders saw the Kushite rulers as potential unifiers who could restore stability and central authority to Egypt.

The conquest of Egypt was finalized by Piye (also known as Piankhi) around 727 BCE, and he established Egypt's Twenty-fifth Dynasty. The Kushite rulers successfully consolidated their power in Egypt, with their authority extending as far north as the Nile Delta. They created a centralized administration and promoted political stability in the regions they controlled.[19]

The Twenty-fifth Dynasty

The Kushites' control of Egypt was made more accessible because of the past centuries of assimilation. Kushite pharaohs revered Egyptian gods and built temples for them, which helped them gain acceptance among the Egyptian population and legitimized their rule. The Kushite rulers also initiated various cultural and building projects during their rule in Egypt. They constructed pyramids, temples, and monuments, contributing to the region's architectural heritage. The new rulers of Egypt wore the double crown of earlier pharaohs.

---

[19] K. Krois. Hirst. (2019, May 12). The Kingdom of Kush: Sub-Saharan African Rulers of the Nile. Retrieved from Thoughtco.com: https://www.thoughtco.com/the-kingdom-of-kush-171464.

Statues of some of the late Twenty-fifth Dynasty pharaohs.
Matthias Gehricke, CC BY-SA 4.0 <https://creativecommons.org/licenses/by-sa/4.0>, via Wikimedia Commons;
https://commons.wikimedia.org/wiki/File:Rulers_of_Kush,_Kerma_Museum.jpg

The Twenty-fifth Dynasty only survived for a short time. The Kushite control of Egypt lasted for several decades, with varying degrees of success. However, their rule eventually faced challenges from the Assyrians, who invaded Egypt in the late 7th century BCE. The Assyrians managed to defeat the Kushite rulers and effectively ended the Twenty-fifth Dynasty's control over Egypt. The Kushites withdrew to their homeland in Kush, and Egypt fell under the control of foreign powers.

Kush continued to be a regional power but grew weaker after the Roman occupation of Egypt. Kush collapsed in the 4th century CE.

In Summary

The Twenty-fifth Dynasty's control of Egypt represented a unique chapter in the history of both regions, demonstrating the fluidity of power in ancient Africa and the influence of neighboring kingdoms. The Kushites left a significant mark on Egyptian history and culture during their rule, and their legacy endures in the archaeological and historical record.

Chapter 4: Aksum

The Kingdom of Aksum, nestled in the northern regions of present-day Ethiopia and Eritrea, is a fascinating chapter in the annals of African history. Flourishing from around the 1st century BCE to the 7th century CE, Aksum is known for its multifaceted and rich civilization, which included the introduction of Christianity to the region and subsequent works of art and architecture.

<u>Commercial Center</u>

Aksum's economy was a powerhouse driven primarily by trade and agriculture, both of which played a pivotal role in the kingdom's rise and prosperity. Aksum's strategic location at the crossroads of significant trade routes made it an ideal hub for commerce. Its position along the Red Sea coast and its control over major ports, such as Adulis, allowed it to dominate maritime trade in the region. To the west, the kingdom had access to the Nile River, enabling inland trade connections with the African interior.

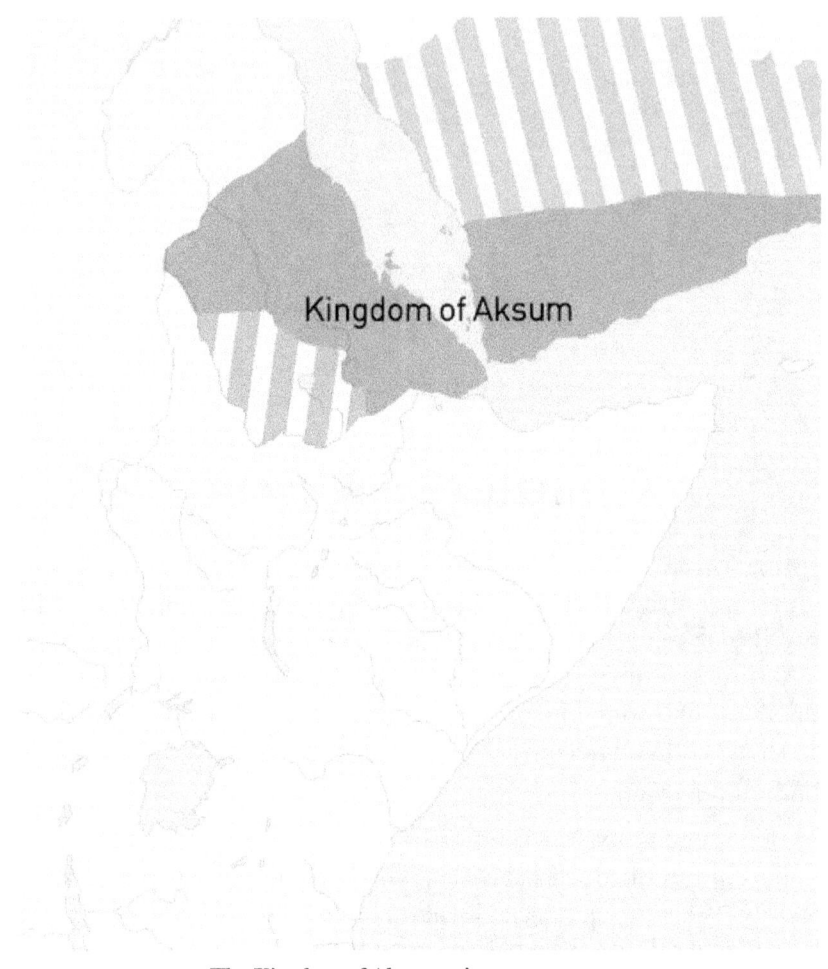

The Kingdom of Aksum at its greatest extent.
Aldan-2, CC BY-SA 4.0 <https://creativecommons.org/licenses/by-sa/4.0>, via Wikimedia Commons; https://commons.wikimedia.org/wiki/File:The_Kingdom_of_Aksum.png

The Red Sea was a vital corridor connecting Africa with the Arabian Peninsula, the Indian subcontinent, and the Mediterranean world. This geographical advantage turned Aksum into a bustling commercial center where goods from distant lands converged.

Aksum engaged in trade with diverse regions, forging economic ties with the Roman Empire, Persia, India, and the Arabian Peninsula. The kingdom's exports included ivory, gold, spices, obsidian, and exotic animals. Among its most prized exports was frankincense, a fragrant gum resin highly sought after in the ancient world. In exchange, Aksum imported luxury items such as textiles, ceramics, glassware, and precious metals. These trade relationships enriched the kingdom and allowed it to accumulate wealth and prestige on the global stage.

Aksum had its own currency system, with gold, silver, and bronze coins. These coins, known as Aksumite coins, served as a medium of exchange within the kingdom and facilitated international trade. The existence of Aksumite coins in various parts of the ancient world is a testament to the kingdom's extensive commercial networks.

Coins of King Ezana.
Classical Numismatic Group, Inc. http://www.cngcoins.com, CC BY-SA 3.0 <http://creativecommons.org/licenses/by-sa/3.0>, via Wikimedia Commons; https://commons.wikimedia.org/wiki/File:AXUM._Ezanas._Circa_330-360.jpg

Agricultural Prowess

Agriculture was vital in ensuring the kingdom's food security and economic stability. Aksum's highlands and plateaus were blessed with fertile soils and favorable rainfall patterns conducive to agriculture. The region's agricultural productivity supported a variety of crops, including millet, barley, wheat, and teff.

The Aksumites were skilled practitioners of terrace farming. This technique involved constructing stepped agricultural platforms on hilly terrain. Terrace farming maximized agricultural output and mitigated soil erosion, ensuring long-term sustainability.[20]

Infrastructure Achievements

Aksum's economic success was not solely reliant on favorable geography and agricultural practices. The kingdom's technological

---

[20] Eries.org. (2024, January 13). Kingdom of Aksum. Retrieved from Eriesd.org:
https://www.eriesd.org/cms/lib/PA01001942/Centricity/Domain/1041/6.2%20The%20Kingdom%20of%20Aksum-1.pdf.

advancements and infrastructure were also crucial.

The Aksumites were pioneers in constructing dams and reservoirs to manage water resources. These structures were critical for irrigation, providing water for crops, and regulating seasonal flooding. The engineering feats of the Aksumites in harnessing and distributing water resources underscored their ability to adapt to the challenges posed by their environment.

Aksum is renowned for its impressive stone architecture, with obelisks, stelae, and monumental structures bearing witness to the kingdom's advanced stonework and engineering skills. The towering obelisks and stelae served various functions, from marking graves to commemorating rulers and their achievements. These monuments also showcased the kingdom's artistic prowess. Some examples of Aksum's impressive obelisks and stelae include the Obelisk of Axum, King Ezana's Stele, and the Great Stele of Axum.

The Obelisk of Axum.
Tesfawel, CC BY-SA 4.0 <https://creativecommons.org/licenses/by-sa/4.0>, via Wikimedia Commons; https://commons.wikimedia.org/wiki/File:Aksum_obelisk.jpg

Social Structure

Understanding Aksumite society is essential to grasp the kingdom's dynamics during its heyday. Aksumite society was hierarchical and characterized by distinct social classes. At the pinnacle stood the ruling elite, comprising the king and the nobility. Below them were freemen and peasants who toiled the land, ensuring the kingdom's agricultural productivity. Slavery was also a part of Aksumite society, with enslaved people primarily acquired through warfare and trade.

Aksum was governed by a monarchy, with the king as the central authority. The Aksumite king's lineage was believed to be traced back to the legendary Queen of Sheba and King Solomon, endowing the monarchy with a strong sense of legitimacy. The kingdom's political structure was centralized, with provinces and local rulers subject to the king's authority.

The Aksumite military was a formidable force, vital for safeguarding trade routes and protecting the kingdom. The kingdom's army included infantry, cavalry, and archers, and it was renowned for its use of war elephants, which provided a significant advantage in battle.

Religion of Aksum

Religion held a central place in Aksumite culture and society, with the kingdom making significant contributions to the early history of Christianity. Aksumites practiced a distinctive form of Christianity known as Ethiopian Orthodox Tewahedo Christianity. The term "Tewahedo" translates as "being made one." It reflects the church's commitment to Orthodox Christian doctrines and its emphasis on unity within the faith. This form of Christianity is still practiced in Ethiopia today.

This faith was pivotal in shaping the Aksumite identity and culture. In the 4th century CE, Christianity was officially adopted as the state religion, making Aksum one of the world's earliest Christian kingdoms.

Ethiopian Orthodox Tewahedo Christianity features distinctive liturgical practices, rituals, and traditions that set it apart from other Christian denominations. The church places significant importance on the Old Testament and emphasizes seven sacraments similar to those observed by the Roman Catholic Church.[21] These include the following:

- Baptism
- Confirmation
- Holy Communion

---

[21] EOTC. (2024, January 13). Beliefs and Teachings of Ethiopian Orthodox Tewahedo Church. Retrieved from keraneyo-medhanealem.com: https://www.keraneyo-medhanealem.com/beliefs-and-origins-7-sacraments-of.

- Ordination
- Holy matrimony
- Mystery of penance
- Unction of the sick.

The Ethiopian Orthodox Church maintains a hierarchical clergy structure, including priests, deacons, and bishops. At the apex of this hierarchy is the Ethiopian patriarch, known as the abuna. The abuna serves as the highest-ranking ecclesiastical authority in the Ethiopian Orthodox Church and plays a crucial role in guiding the spiritual life of the faithful.

Churches and monasteries are central features of religious life. Some of the most notable Aksumite churches are rock-hewn churches, such as the iconic rock-hewn churches of Lalibela. Monasticism also plays a vital role in Ethiopian orthodoxy, with monks and monastic communities preserving religious traditions and manuscripts.

One of the rock-hewn churches in Lalibela.
Bernard Gagnon, CC BY-SA 3.0 <https://creativecommons.org/licenses/by-sa/3.0>, via Wikimedia Commons; https://commons.wikimedia.org/wiki/File:Bete_Abba_Libanos.jpg

The Ethiopian Orthodox Church continues to thrive and exerts a powerful influence in the modern era. The faith remains an integral part of Ethiopia and Eritrea's religious, cultural, and social life. It has contributed to preserving ancient Christian traditions, religious manuscripts, and a vibrant ecclesiastical heritage.

The History of Ancient Aksum

The history of ancient Aksum spanned several centuries, during which time the kingdom witnessed a succession of monarchs and underwent significant transformations. Before the official establishment of the Kingdom of Aksum, the region had a pre-Aksumite history marked by legendary figures and early rulers. This period, dating from approximately the 4th century BCE to the 1st century CE, contributed to the customs, governing patterns, and traditions that laid the foundation for what would later become Aksum.

As Aksum emerged as a significant regional power during the 1st century CE, the lineage of its rulers began to gain historical prominence. A mighty king in the history of Aksum was Ezana.[22]

Ezana and the Conversion

The 4th century CE is a watershed moment in Aksumite history, as this was the century when Christianity was officially adopted as the state religion. The early adoption of Christianity in Aksum holds immense historical significance. It predates the Christianization of other prominent regions in the world, including the Roman Empire, challenging Eurocentric narratives and emphasizing Africa's central role in the early history of Christianity.

This period witnessed the reign of King Ezana, a monarch whose legacy is intimately tied to the kingdom's religious transformation. Ezana's reign, which extended from 333 to 356 CE, was a turning point for Aksum. His most significant contribution was his conversion to Christianity, an event documented in inscriptions, including the renowned Stele of Ezana. It is a monumental obelisk bearing inscriptions in Ge'ez, the ancient Ethiopian script.

---

[22] Cartwright, M. (2019, March 21). Kingdom of Axum. Retrieved from Worldhistory.org: https://www.worldhistory.org/Kingdom_of_Axum/.

Stele of Ezana.
Sailko, CC BY 3.0 <https://creativecommons.org/licenses/by/3.0>, via Wikimedia Commons;
https://commons.wikimedia.org/wiki/File:Aksum,_stele_3_detta_di_re_ezana,_1%27unica_mai_c
rollata_04.jpg

The Kingdom's Golden Age

The centuries following Aksum's conversion to Christianity marked a golden age for the kingdom. It reached its zenith of power, conducted campaigns for territorial expansion, and created enduring cultural achievements.

King Kaleb (r. 514–542) stands out as one of the most influential rulers of this era. Under his leadership, Aksum expanded its territories into the Arabian Peninsula. His reign was marked by military campaigns and diplomatic achievements that solidified Aksum's status as a regional powerhouse.

The Decline and Fall of Aksum

The 7th century CE marked the beginning of Aksum's decline. Factors contributing to this decline included the rise of Islam, which disrupted Aksum's traditional trade routes, and internal conflicts within the kingdom. As the once-mighty kingdom faced mounting challenges, it began to recede from its prominent position in the region.

Environmental factors played a pivotal role in the decline of Aksum as well. One of the primary concerns was environmental degradation, including deforestation and soil erosion. The kingdom's ability to sustain its population and support its economy was severely hampered.

Aksum's prosperity was intricately linked to its role as a significant trading empire. However, the alteration of global trade routes, particularly the redirection of commerce away from the Red Sea, posed a significant threat to Aksum's economic stability. New maritime routes circumventing Aksum emerged, leading to decreased regional trade activity. As a result, Aksum began to lose its prominence as a trade hub, affecting its economic vitality.

The economic decline of Aksum was a multifaceted issue. Reduced agricultural output and a drop in trade revenue left Aksum in a precarious financial position. The kingdom struggled to maintain its infrastructure, support its military, and fund its administrative institutions. As Aksum's resources diminished, its ability to engage in large-scale architectural projects waned, reflecting its declining power and prestige.[23]

To assert that Islam harmed Aksum oversimplifies a nuanced historical narrative. The relationship between the Aksumite Kingdom and early Islam in the Horn of Africa is a complex aspect of history. It is crucial to consider the chronological context, the dynamics of religious transformation, economic factors, and competition.

While there were periods of peaceful coexistence and cooperation, there were also conflicts and tensions between the Aksumite Kingdom and early Muslim communities. These conflicts often arose due to

---

[23] Iniguez, N. (2020, February 28). The Rise, Decline, and Collapse of the Aksum Empire. Retrieved from Storymaps.arcgis.com:
https://storymaps.arcgis.com/stories/9b7b377398724be99a0d94dfa9f55550.

territorial disputes, competition over trade routes, and religious differences. Some historians have noted clashes along the Red Sea coast as a result of these factors.

Political instability, including internal conflicts and disputes over succession, plagued Aksum during its later years. A lack of strong and cohesive leadership made it difficult for the kingdom to address its various challenges effectively. The absence of effective governance exacerbated the kingdom's vulnerabilities, leaving it ill-prepared to confront external threats and internal strife. While the exact chronology of events remains a subject of historical inquiry, it is clear that Aksum faced formidable challenges that tested its resilience.

In Summary

The history of the Kingdom of Aksum is a remarkable tale woven with the reigns of monarchs and the milestones they achieved. From its pre-Aksumite origins and the emergence of regional power to its conversion to Christianity and the golden age of expansion and cultural achievement, Aksum's history is a testament to the dynamism of African civilizations.

Chapter 5: Punt: A Faraway Land?

The Land of Punt, often referred to as the "Land of God," occupies a unique place in the annals of ancient history. This enigmatic land, known for its production and trade of valuable commodities such as gold, ebony, myrrh, and exotic animals, has captured the imagination of scholars, Egyptologists, historians, and many others for centuries. However, whether Punt was a real place or merely an El Dorado-like myth has been a subject of ongoing debate and intrigue.

We are going to investigate the arguments both for and against the existence of Punt, with a focus on evidence like archaeological findings, historical records, and stories and legends.

Archaeological Discoveries

Archaeological evidence forms a cornerstone in the argument for the existence of Punt. Ancient Egyptian hieroglyphs and inscriptions frequently mention Punt, its people, and their distinctive attire and features. These references underscore Punt's role in Egyptian culture and its enduring presence in historical records. Various discoveries provide tangible proof of Punt's existence and its historical interactions with ancient civilizations.

- The Palermo Stone is an inscription that provides clues that suggest there was a place called Punt. The Palermo Stone dates from Egypt's Old Kingdom period (c. 2500 BCE). It documents an expedition sent by Pharoah Sahure. The expedition fleet brought back a large cargo of myrrh, malachite, electrum, and wood (possibly ebony). The Palermo Stone is the first documented evidence that Punt existed. Unfortunately, it does not tell where Punt is located.

The Palermo Stone.
No restrictions;
https://commons.wikimedia.org/wiki/File:Abhandlungen_der_K%C3%B6niglich_Preussischen_Akademie_der_Wissenschaften_aus_dem_Jahre_(1902)_(16765759871).jpg

- The mortuary temple of Queen Hatshepsut at Deir el-Bahri, constructed during the 15th century BCE, contains intricate reliefs and inscriptions that offer a vivid account of the expedition to Punt during her reign. These inscriptions detail the exotic flora and fauna encountered during the journey, providing tangible evidence of Punt's biodiversity. The goods obtained from Punt, including myrrh, ebony, and incense trees, are depicted, reinforcing the reality of trade between Egypt and Punt. There is no indication on the temple walls where Punt can be found on a map, though.

- The temple complex at Medinet Habu, dating to the 12th century BCE and built during the reign of Pharaoh Ramesses III, is another significant archaeological source. Inscriptions and reliefs at this site corroborate the existence of Punt and the trade relationships between the two regions. A papyrus scroll describes the transport vessels bringing back goods from Punt. Still, there is no mention of the exact location of this land.
- Punt has left tantalizing linguistic evidence that adds depth to the debate surrounding its historical existence. While linguistic evidence alone may not definitively prove the existence of the Land of Punt, it serves as a critical piece of the puzzle in understanding the land's potential reality.

Hieroglyphs provide some of the best linguistic evidence. Punt is prominently featured in numerous Egyptian texts and inscriptions, particularly during the reign of Queen Hatshepsut. These inscriptions not only mention Punt but also describe the Puntites' customs and the valuable resources obtained from the land. The hieroglyphic texts often include distinctive symbols that signify Punt's location. Although they do not provide precise geographical coordinates, they are linguistic markers that link Punt to the rich tapestry of Egyptian records. The Somali language has similarities with ancient Egyptian vocabulary, suggesting a relationship between the Horn of Africa and the Land of the Pharaohs.[24]

The Words of the Bible

The biblical references to Punt contribute indirectly to the argument for its existence. The Old Testament mentions Ophir as a land associated with the trade of gold and other precious commodities, which aligns with the historical descriptions of Punt. The Old Testament includes the following verses that mention Ophir:

---

[24] Team, E. (2018, October 21). Kingdom of Punt: When Ancient Egypt Envied Somalia. Retrieved from Thinkafrica.net: https://thinkafrica.net/land-of-punt/.

Genesis 10:29:

"And Ophir, and Havilah, and Jobab; all these were the sons of Joktan."

1 Kings 9:28:

"And they came to Ophir and fetched from thence gold, four hundred and twenty talents, and brought it to King Solomon."

1 Kings 10:11:

"And the navy also of Hiram, that brought gold from Ophir, brought in from Ophir great plenty of almug trees and precious stones."

1 Chronicles 29:4:

"Even three thousand talents of gold, of the gold of Ophir, and seven thousand talents of refined silver, to overlay the walls of the houses withal."

Job 22:24:

"Then shalt thou lay up gold as dust, and the gold of Ophir as the stones of the brooks."

1 Kings 9:26-28 gives ancient geographical context about Ophir's possible location. It might have been a land bordering on the Red Sea.

"King Solomon also built ships at Ezion Geber, which is near Elath in Edom, on the shore of the Red Sea. And Hiram sent his men—sailors who knew the sea—to serve in the fleet with Solomon's men. They sailed to Ophir and brought back 420 talents of gold, which they delivered to King Solomon."[25]

Whether Ophir and Punt are the same or if they were part of a broader trading network remains a subject of ongoing research and debate. As archaeological discoveries and linguistic studies advance, we may uncover more definitive evidence regarding the historical relationship between these enigmatic lands. The historical prominence of the Red Sea as a trade route has led some researchers to propose that Ophir and Punt could have been part of a broader trading network that extended across these regions.

<u>The Queen's Expedition</u>

The history of ancient Egypt is replete with remarkable pharaohs and monumental events. Still, few are as intriguing and enigmatic as Queen

---

[25] https://www.biblegateway.com/versions/New-International-Version-NIV-Bible/

Hatshepsut and her expedition to Punt and the subsequent suppression of her legacy by her successor, Thutmose III. Queen Hatshepsut, one of Egypt's few female pharaohs, ascended to the throne during the Eighteenth Dynasty, approximately around 1479 BCE.

Queen Hatshepsut's reign was characterized by a keen desire to secure the prosperity and stability of Egypt. She recognized that access to valuable resources and strengthening trade relationships with other lands were essential. One of her most notable initiatives was the expedition to Punt.

The motivation behind this expedition was twofold. Firstly, Punt was renowned for its valuable resources, including myrrh, frankincense, ebony, and exotic animals. These commodities held immense value in the ancient world for their economic worth, use in religious rituals, and as symbols of power and prestige. Secondly, Queen Hatshepsut aimed to strengthen Egypt's diplomatic and trade ties with the Land of Punt, thereby enhancing her kingdom's economic and political influence in the region.

Queen Hatshepsut's expedition to Punt was documented in an artistic detail that has survived thousands of years. Her mortuary temple at Deir el-Bahri, located on the west bank of the Nile River, is adorned with vivid and intricate reliefs and inscriptions that depict facets of the Punt expedition.

The meticulousness of these records is a testament to the importance Queen Hatshepsut placed on documenting her accomplishments and the significance of her trade mission to Punt.

The inscriptions provide a treasure of information about the journey, including the exotic flora and fauna encountered, the unique customs and attire of the Puntites, and the goods obtained during the expedition.

The goods obtained from Punt during the expedition held immense value in ancient Egypt. Myrrh and frankincense, obtained from the resin of trees native to Punt, were essential in religious rituals and highly prized for their fragrance and symbolic significance. Ebony, another notable resource, was used to craft luxurious furniture and decorative items, further enhancing the pharaoh's prestige and the kingdom's material wealth.

The acquisition of exotic animals during the Punt expedition also contributed to Egypt's zoological diversity. Scenes from the reliefs at Deir el-Bahri depict the transportation of baboons, cheetahs, giraffes, and other animals to Egypt. These additions to the Egyptian royal menagerie were a testament to Queen Hatshepsut's success in Punt and a display of her power.

The inscriptions and reliefs at Deir el-Bahri depict scenes of exchange, gift-giving, and friendly interactions between the Egyptians and the people of Punt. These depictions emphasize the diplomatic nature of the mission and the desire to foster positive relations.

The Punt expedition allowed Egypt to secure valuable resources and establish itself as a dominant player in the Red Sea trade networks.[26]

The Suppression of Queen Hatshepsut's Legacy

Upon Queen Hatshepsut's death, her stepson Thutmose III assumed the throne. While Hatshepsut's reign was groundbreaking, her status as a female pharaoh raised complex issues of legitimacy. Thutmose III initiated a campaign to erase her legacy from the historical record.

Perhaps the most iconic example of Thutmose III's efforts to suppress Queen Hatshepsut's legacy can be seen at her mortuary temple at Deir el-Bahri. The walls of this temple, which had been adorned with vivid reliefs and inscriptions commemorating her reign and the Punt expedition, bear clear signs of deliberate defacement. Queen Hatshepsut's image was chiseled away. Her name was erased, and her accomplishments were obscured.

Despite Thutmose III's efforts, Queen Hatshepsut's legacy was not entirely obliterated. In modern times, Egyptologists and archaeologists have successfully reconstructed her history and accomplishments through meticulous research and deciphering ancient inscriptions. The expedition to Punt is one of the queen's most outstanding achievements, which a stone mason's chisel could not obliterate.

The Myth

The ongoing debate over the exact location of Punt has helped perpetuate its mythic allure. Punt's mythical aura was partly born from its immense wealth and the exotic nature of the goods it provided.

In the ancient Egyptian mindset, Punt symbolized a distant and idealized source of wealth and luxury. Punt's portrayal as a foreign and exotic land, as seen in Egyptian inscriptions and reliefs, further solidified

---

[26] Tyson, P. (2009, December 1). Where is Punt? Retrieved from PBS.org: https://www.pbs.org/wgbh/nova/article/egypt-punt/.

its mythical status. The people of Punt were often depicted with unique clothing and physical features, enhancing the image of an otherworldly realm. Gold, one of Punt's most coveted commodities, held a special place in the ancient world, signifying power, prestige, and divine favor. Punt's association with gold contributed to its mythical status.

The presence of linguistic and cultural influences between the peoples of the Red Sea and East African regions and the biblical narrative adds to the complexity of the debate. Exploring lesser-known indigenous accounts and oral traditions from these regions may provide insights into their historical connections with Ophir (Punt).

A Compelling Clue

Archaeology is an ongoing study of the past, and it frequently exposes evidence that has been buried for thousands of years. These uncovered facts can lead to amazing discoveries that will identify missing links. We may be closer to identifying the location of Punt thanks to the remains of a band of monkeys.

Nathaniel Dominy is an anthropologist at Dartmouth College studying isotopes of strontium and oxygen taken from mummified baboons of Egypt's New Kingdom era (c. 1550-1069 BCE). His research led him to discover that some of the animal remains were not Egyptian but came from the Horn of Africa region. This is an important discovery because the records show that Egyptians obtained baboons from Punt.

Gisela Kopp, an evolutionary biologist from the University of Konstanz, found evidence in another mummified baboon that the animal's point of origin might have been along the Red Sea coast. Both researchers believe that the baboons originated in the area of the seaport Adulis, which is in modern Eritrea.[27]

What does this mean? One possibility is that Adulis was the contact point between Egypt and Punt. Goods coming from the interior might have been traded on the port docks. It is also possible that there was no Kingdom of Punt. Instead, there could have been a city-state that had extensive trade relations with Egypt.

---

[27] Mummified Baboons Point to the Direction of the Fabled Land of Punt. (2023, November 11). Retrieved from Ars Technical: https://arstechnica.com/science/2023/11/mummified-baboons-point-to-the-direction-of-the-fabled-land-of-punt/.

What is significant about this research is that it helps narrow down where Punt might have been. Baboons were revered in ancient Egyptian religion, and being able to purchase them would have been important to them. Obtaining these animals may have led to further trade, including the exotic commodities Egyptian expeditions brought home.[28]

<u>In Summary</u>

The evidence for and against Punt's existence presents a complex picture. Archaeological discoveries, including temple reliefs, inscriptions, and botanical remains, provide tangible proof of Punt's historical existence and its role in trade networks. Linguistic and cultural references reinforce the reality of Punt's presence in the ancient world. Ongoing archaeological research in the Red Sea and Horn of Africa regions continues to uncover new evidence that may shed light on the historical trade relationships and the locations of ancient civilizations, including Punt and possibly Ophir.

Punt represents a blend of historical reality and mythic elements that have grown around it over time, making it a subject of enduring fascination and exploration in ancient African history. Was it a real place on the map, or is Punt simply a legend of a fabulously wealthy country? Based on facts and stories, the best answer is that Punt is a little bit of both.

---

[28] Fitzgerald, S. (2023, November 21). Mummified Baboons in Egypt Point to a Long Lost Land. Retrieved from Atlas Obscura: https://www.atlasobscura.com/articles/mummified-baboons-punt.

Part 3: The Great Empires and Their Legacies

Chapter 6: Ancient Egypt

A book on ancient Africa has to include Egypt. It was the premier culture on the continent for centuries, and it still fascinates us to this day. People know quite a bit about the political and military history of the land of the pharaohs, and we will, of course, talk about it. However, we will also explore some lesser-known accomplishments that were just as significant.

Egypt's history is divided into four primary eras: the Old Kingdom, the Middle Kingdom, the New Kingdom, and the Ptolemaic era. We will discuss each one in sequence.

<u>The Old Kingdom (c. 2686-2181 BCE)</u>

The Old Kingdom represents a remarkable period in human history, especially in terms of its scientific achievements. This era, often called the Age of the Pyramids, was marked by significant advancements in various fields.

<u>Science</u>
- Astronomy and Mathematics:

  The Egyptians of the Old Kingdom developed a calendar based on their observations of the star Sirius and the annual flooding of the Nile. This lunar calendar was crucial for agricultural planning. Their understanding of geometry was essential for land surveying, especially after the Nile floods, and for the architectural planning of pyramids. Astronomical observations also played a significant role in religious practices. The movement of stars and celestial events were often interpreted as divine messages.[29]

- Engineering and Architecture:

The most outstanding scientific achievements of the Old Kingdom are undoubtedly the construction of the pyramids, especially the Great Pyramid of Giza. These structures are not just architectural marvels but also a testament to the Egyptians' advanced understanding of engineering principles. The pyramids demonstrate an advanced knowledge of engineering and mathematics.[30]

Those who believe in extraterrestrial beings are convinced the pyramids were built by aliens. There is, of course, no plausible evidence to support the assumption. The Egyptians gradually learned through trial and error how to construct these edifices (for instance, the Step Pyramid of Djoser, which was built earlier). The pyramids also demonstrate that Africa was not a primitive continent. The inhabitants were capable of astounding achievements.

The pyramids of Giza.
Ricardo Liberato, CC BY-SA 2.0 <https://creativecommons.org/licenses/by-sa/2.0>, via Wikimedia Commons; https://commons.wikimedia.org/wiki/File:All_Gizah_Pyramids-2.jpg

---

[29] Wendorg, M. (2023, April 23). Ancient Egyptian Technology and Inventions. Retrieved from Interesting Enginerring.com: https://interestingengineering.com/lists/ancient-egyptian-technology-and-inventions.

[30] Mark, J. J. (2016, November 9). Ancient Egyptian Science & Technology. Retrieved from World History Encyclopedia: https://www.worldhistory.org/article/967/ancient-egyptian-science-technology/.

- **Medical Practices:**

  The Egyptians had a basic understanding of anatomy, pharmacology, and possibly even surgical practices. The Edwin Smith Papyrus was written during the Middle Kingdom, but this work is considered a copy of much earlier texts. There is evidence of significant medical knowledge during the Old Kingdom.

  Egyptian medicine in the Old Kingdom included various herbs and other natural substances for treating ailments. There was also an understanding of surgical procedures, as evidenced by surgical instruments found at archaeological sites. Institutions known as "Houses of Life" had medical purposes and existed in the First Dynasty.

Economics

Advances in agriculture were crucial for maintaining a prosperous economy. The Egyptians developed sophisticated irrigation systems to control the flooding of the Nile, which allowed for consistent agricultural production. In addition to irrigation canals to manage the flow of the Nile's waters, the Egyptians invented a water wheel, the *shadoof*, to transfer water into a canal.

There was also an expansion in the variety of crops grown, including the introduction of new grains and fruits, which contributed to a more stable and varied food supply.

Egypt's agricultural economy enabled it to become a powerful economic force in the ancient world. The Old Kingdom saw the establishment of extensive trade networks, both within Egypt and with neighboring regions like Nubia, the Levant, and the Mediterranean. These trade networks helped in the acquisition of luxury goods and building materials not available locally. The ability to navigate the Nile and the seas opened Egypt up to a world of trade, cultural exchange, and military expeditions.[31]

---

[31] Historyskills.com. (2024, January 19). How Egypt Became the Greatest Superpower of the Ancient World. Retrieved from Hisoryskills.com:
https://www.historyskills.com/classroom/ancient-history/egypt-ancient-superpower/.

Politics and Society

The Old Kingdom created a strong, centralized state governed by the pharaoh. The concept of the pharaoh as a god-king was solidified during this time. This notion reinforced the political structure, as the pharaoh's absolute authority was seen as divinely ordained. This period saw the development of an efficient bureaucracy that was essential for managing large-scale projects, tax collection, and administration.

The Old Kingdom had a social hierarchy with the pharaoh at the top, followed by nobles, priests, artisans, and farmers. The bottom rung of society was occupied by slaves. This hierarchy was integral to the functioning of society. If someone stepped out of their designed social role, the Egyptians believed it would bring disharmony to Egypt and cause chaos.[32]

This era significantly saw developments in Egyptian art, literature, and religious practices. The construction of pyramids and large tombs decorated with intricate art and hieroglyphs reflects the period's cultural richness. Writing was, without a doubt, the most significant educational innovation of the Old Kingdom. The Egyptian writing system included two thousand hieroglyphic symbols and an alphabet.[33]

Most Important Pharaohs

Several pharaohs played pivotal roles in shaping Egyptian history during the Old Kingdom. Their reigns were marked by significant accomplishments, particularly in architecture, administration, and religious practices. Here are some of the most prominent pharaohs from this period:

- Djoser (c. 2630–2611 BCE)

Djoser, the second pharaoh of the Third Dynasty, is best known for his step pyramid at Saqqara. This pyramid, designed by his vizier Imhotep, is considered one of the earliest large-scale cut-stone constructions. It marked a significant advancement from the traditional mastaba tombs and set the precedent for later pyramid construction.

---

[32] Mark, J. J. (2017, September 21). Social Structure in Ancient Egypt. Retrieved from History World Encyclopedia: https://www.worldhistory.org/article/1123/social-structure-in-ancient-egypt/.

[33] Lifepersona.com. (2024, January 19). The 9 Most Important Contributions of Egypt to Humanity. Retrieved from Lifepersona.com: https://www.lifepersona.com/the-9-most-important-contributions-of-egypt-to-humanity.

Step Pyramid of Djoser.
Charles J. Sharp, CC BY-SA 3.0 <https://creativecommons.org/licenses/by-sa/3.0>, via Wikimedia Commons; https://commons.wikimedia.org/wiki/File:Saqqara_pyramid_ver_2.jpg

- Sneferu (c. 2575-2551 BCE)

Sneferu, the founder of the Fourth Dynasty, was an incredibly prolific pyramid builder. He is credited with building three major pyramids: the Meidum Pyramid, the Bent Pyramid, and the Red Pyramid. These structures represent important stages in the evolution of pyramid construction, culminating in the Red Pyramid, Egypt's first successful attempt at a true smooth-sided pyramid.

- Khufu (c. 2589-2566 BCE)

Sneferu's successor, Khufu, is best known for the Great Pyramid of Giza, one of the Seven Wonders of the Ancient World. This colossal structure exemplifies the architectural skill and organizational ability of the Old Kingdom and remains a testament to the Egyptians' engineering prowess.

- Khafre (Chephren) (c. 2558-2532 BCE)

Khafre, Khufu's son, built the second-largest pyramid at Giza. He is also credited with the construction of the Sphinx, a monumental limestone statue with the body of a lion and a pharaoh's head, likely intended to be a likeness of Khafre himself.

- Menkaure (c. 2532-2503 BCE)

Menkaure, another son of Khufu, is known for constructing the third and smallest of the Giza pyramids. Although smaller, this pyramid is notable for its complex mortuary temple and exquisite craftsmanship.

- Pepi II (c. 2278-2184 BCE)

Pepi II, who ascended to the throne as a young boy, is believed to have reigned for ninety-four years, the longest of any Egyptian pharaoh. His reign eventually led to internal trouble in the government and the civil wars that marked the end of the Old Kingdom.

These pharaohs were instrumental in establishing many of the defining characteristics of ancient Egyptian civilization. The pyramids, in particular, stand as enduring symbols of the Old Kingdom's grandeur and the pharaohs' quest for immortality.

The Middle Kingdom (c. 2030-1650 BCE)

There was turmoil in Egypt after the Old Kingdom came to an end. However, Egypt was able to rebound from internal strife and enter into a period that was one of its greatest: the Middle Kingdom.

While the Middle Kingdom has often been overlooked by the achievements of the Old and New Kingdoms, it was a pivotal chapter in the ancient Egyptian narrative.

Mathematics

We should remember that the Middle Kingdom was built on breakthroughs that took place in the Old Kingdom, so many innovations were logical progressions of what came before. There is documentation from the Twelfth Dynasty that shows an interest in the use of fractions. Papyrus documents, such as the Moscow Mathematics Papyrus and the Egyptian Mathematical Leather Roll, date to the Middle Kingdom. Mathematical problem tests, including solutions, come from this Egyptian era as well. These suggest a practical approach to mathematics as opposed to a theoretical one. Fractions were essential for temple and pyramid construction and were used in the complex task of managing the nation's granaries and resources.

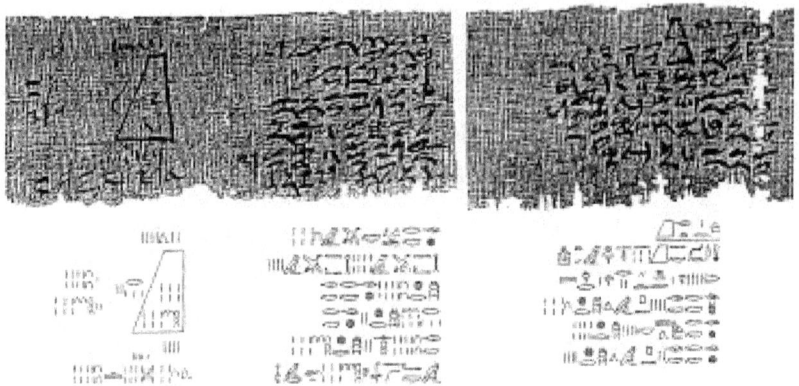

A mathematical problem in the Moscow Mathematics Papyrus.
https://commons.wikimedia.org/wiki/File:Moskou-papyrus.jpg

Architecture and Shipbuilding

The Middle Kingdom of Egypt was a time of political stability and cultural flourishing, which is vividly reflected in the era's architectural and maritime innovations.

Pyramids were still being built, although the building material gradually went from solid stone to mud brick with a limestone casing. The pyramids were no longer the burial chamber of choice by the end of the Twelfth Dynasty. Rock-cut tombs in the Valley of Kings and the Valley of Queens were used instead. What is interesting is the use of rudimentary urban planning in the construction of workers' villages near the burial construction sites.

Architecture became refined during the Twelfth Dynasty. The Karnak Temple Complex, especially the White Chapel, exemplified the new building styles.[34]

---

[34] Brewminate.com. (2019, April 17). The Art and Architecture of Middle Kingdom Egypt c. 2055-1650 BCE. Retrieved from brewminate.com: https://brewminate.com/the-art-and-architecture-of-middle-kingdom-egypt-c-2055-1650-bce/.

Pillars of the Great Hypostyle Hall at Karnak.
René Hourdry, CC BY-SA 4.0 <https://creativecommons.org/licenses/by-sa/4.0>, via Wikimedia Commons; https://commons.wikimedia.org/wiki/File:Temple_de_Louxor_68.jpg

The construction of large seaworthy vessels opened new possibilities for trade, military campaigns, and mining expeditions. These ships enabled the Egyptians to extend their influence and secure resources from distant lands, which was crucial for the kingdom's economy and position in the ancient world.

References such as the "Tale of the Shipwrecked Sailor" suggest the construction of large ships designed for long voyages, indicating an advanced understanding of shipbuilding. The design and function of these ships were likely tailored for specific purposes, reflecting a sophisticated knowledge of maritime engineering and the diverse needs of Egyptian society during this period.

While specific details on the materials and techniques are scarce, the Egyptians' tradition of shipbuilding and their access to quality timbers suggest a high level of craftsmanship. The use of cedar from Lebanon, known for its durability and strength, would have been pivotal in constructing sturdy and seaworthy vessels.

Society

The Middle Kingdom marked a transition toward a more centralized and efficient government compared to the Old Kingdom. A robust bureaucracy was developed, which was crucial in managing the country's resources, executing large-scale construction projects, and maintaining administrative order.

Additionally, this era is noted for legal reforms. The laws were more organized and codified than in the earlier periods, which helped maintain social order and justice. These reforms were essential in stabilizing a society that had experienced significant turmoil.

During the Middle Kingdom, there was a rise in the prominence and influence of the middle class, including artisans, scribes, and officials. This period is often characterized by a degree of social mobility, which contrasted to the more rigidly hierarchical structure of the Old Kingdom.

Arts and Culture

The Middle Kingdom is celebrated for its literary and artistic achievements. Literature from this period, including works like "The Tale of Sinuhe" and the "Instructions of Amenemhat," is renowned for its sophistication and depth. These works not only provide insight into the culture and societal values of the time but also reflect the intellectual and artistic endeavors of the Middle Kingdom.

Craftsmanship and industry also saw remarkable growth during this time. The period was known for its exquisite jewelry, pottery, and statues. These advancements were aesthetic and technological, reflecting a deeper understanding of materials and techniques. The skills and practices developed during this period laid the foundation for the artistic achievements of the later New Kingdom.

One of the most striking features of Middle Kingdom art was the shift toward realism. Unlike the idealized forms of the Old Kingdom, the art of this era depicted figures with more individualistic and realistic features. This change is evident in the portrayal of pharaohs, where their solemnity and individual characteristics are more pronounced, as seen in the sculptures of Senusret III. Block statues, a new form of sculpture, emerged during this period. These statues typically depicted a squatting figure with their knees drawn up to their chest and were often inscribed with autobiographical texts or hymns, adding a personal dimension to the art.

Statue of Senusret III located in the British Museum.
British Museum, CC BY-SA 3.0 <http://creativecommons.org/licenses/by-sa/3.0>, via Wikimedia Commons; https://commons.wikimedia.org/wiki/File:StatueOfSesotrisIII-EA684-BritishMuseum-August19-08.jpg

Funerary art included items such as shabtis and scarabs. Shabtis were small figurines intended to serve the deceased in the afterlife, while scarabs were amulets believed to protect against dangers in the afterlife.

The Middle Kingdom also saw an increase in the representation and patronage of art by women. This is exemplified in the sculpture of a noblewoman from the Twelfth Dynasty, indicating a respected status for women in society and their active participation in the cultural domain.[35]

The art of the Middle Kingdom, with its shift toward realism, inclusion of diverse social classes, and incorporation of personal and symbolic elements, offers invaluable insights into the lives and beliefs of the ancient Egyptians during this transformative period. The legacy of Middle Kingdom art, therefore, lies not only in its aesthetic achievements but also in its reflection of a society in the midst of profound change.

Economics and Politics

The Middle Kingdom was a period of considerable economic expansion and prosperity. This era saw a significant increase in trade, both internally and with foreign lands. Trade routes were established and expanded with neighboring regions and possibly even with distant lands like the Aegean region and Mesopotamia. Exotic goods like gold, copper, lapis lazuli, and cedar wood, essential for temple and tomb constructions, were commonly traded items.

Trade routes extended to far-flung regions, enabling the exchange of goods like spices, perfumes, gold, and jewels. This trade took place over land and sea routes, thereby broadening Egypt's commercial reach. Markets in towns and villages became bustling centers of commerce, facilitating the exchange of goods and contributing to the diversification of the economy. Trade also introduced banking and money-lending services, often involving commodities like grain or salt.

The foundation of the Middle Kingdom's economy was its agricultural sector. Blessed with the fertile lands of the Nile Valley, the Egyptians cultivated crops like wheat, barley, and various vegetables. The Nile's annual flooding ensured rich, arable land, supporting a growing population and allowing surplus production.[36]

The construction of grand temples and monuments served religious and cultural purposes and stimulated the economy through the utilization of vast labor forces and resources. These projects provided

---

[35] Pressbooks.bccampus.ca. (2024, January 19). Middle Kingdom Art. Retrieved from Art and Visual Culture: Prehistory to Renaissance: https://pressbooks.bccampus.ca/cavestocathedrals/chapter/middle-kingdom/.

[36] Cassar, C. (2023, August 25). Exploring the Egyptian Middle Kingdom—A Historical Overview. Retrieved from Anthropologureview.org: https://anthropologyreview.org/history/ancient-egypt/exploring-the-egyptian-middle-kingdom-a-historical-overview/?expand_article=1.

employment for a large number of workers. The emphasis on preparing for the afterlife, manifested in elaborate burial practices and tomb constructions, further contributed to economic activities, especially in funerary goods and services industries.[37]

Military Expansion

The Middle Kingdom commenced with the reunification of Egypt under Mentuhotep II. He was a warrior pharaoh who reconsolidated the fragmented nation and initiated a series of military campaigns, particularly in the northwest Sinai region and Nubia.

War played a major role in Egypt's economic aspirations. Pharaohs like Amenemhat III launched successful campaigns against neighboring territories, increasing Egypt's wealth and power. Egypt's control over a more extensive territory allowed for greater economic stability and the accumulation of wealth. Establishing military fortresses, like the one in the region of Elephantine, was crucial in maintaining control over these acquired territories.[38]

The Mighty Pharaohs

The Middle Kingdom heralded a phase of political consolidation, cultural renaissance, and economic prosperity. The reigns of several pharaohs allowed this to happen.

- Mentuhotep II (c. 2061-2010 BCE)

    The Middle Kingdom started during the reign of Mentuhotep II. As we just mentioned, he was the pharaoh who reunified Egypt. After a prolonged period of disunity and chaos, Mentuhotep II defeated the rival Tenth Dynasty of Hierakonpolis, ending the First Intermediate Period. This reunification restored political stability and set the stage for a cultural and economic revival.

    Mentuhotep II was a patron of the arts and architecture. His mortuary complex in Deir el-Bahri, near Thebes, is a testament

---

[37] Cassar, C. (2023, August 25). Exploring the Egyptian Middle Kingdom—A Historical Overview. Retrieved from Anthropologureview.org: https://anthropologyreview.org/history/ancient-egypt/exploring-the-egyptian-middle-kingdom-a-historical-overview/?expand_article=1.

[38] Historyskills.com. (2024, January 19). What Was the Middle Kingdom of Ancient Egypt? Retrieved from Historyskills.com: https://www.historyskills.com/classroom/ancient-history/anc-middle-kingdom-reading/.

to the architectural innovations made under his reign. This complex, which predates the famous temple of Hatshepsut, showcases a unique architectural style that blended elements of traditional mastaba tombs with those of pyramidal structures, setting a precedent for future temples in Egypt.

- Amenemhat I (c. 1991-1962 BCE)

   The start of the Twelfth Dynasty under Amenemhat I marked the beginning of what is often considered the golden age of the Middle Kingdom. One of Amenemhat's first actions as pharaoh was to move the capital from Thebes to a new city, Itjtawy, which is believed to be located near the pharaoh's burial site in Faiyum. This strategic relocation facilitated better control over the kingdom and symbolized a new era in Egyptian history.

   Amenemhat I's reign was characterized by significant administrative and economic reforms. He initiated projects to increase agricultural productivity, particularly in the Faiyum region, which became a central agricultural hub under his rule. Moreover, his military campaigns to secure Egypt's northeastern borders were crucial in safeguarding the nation against potential Asiatic invasions, thereby ensuring the stability and security of his reign.

- Senusret I (c. 1971-1926 BCE)

   Senusret I, also known as Sesostris I, was originally a co-regent with his father Amenemhat I and reigned from approximately 1971 to 1926 BCE. He expanded Egyptian influence into Nubia and the Near East through a series of successful military campaigns. These campaigns secured Egypt's borders and provided access to critical trade routes and resources, further bolstering the kingdom's economy.

   Senusret I was a great patron of the arts. His reign saw a significant flourishing of artistic expression, with an emphasis on the construction of temples and shrines. The arts, particularly sculpture and relief work, saw remarkable advancements during his reign, characterized by a sense of realism and attention to detail not seen in previous eras. This cultural renaissance under Senusret I significantly contributed to the legacy of the Middle Kingdom as a period of heightened artistic and cultural activity.

- Amenemhat III (c. 1860-1814 BCE)

Amenemhat III's reign is often considered the zenith of the Middle Kingdom in terms of economic prosperity and architectural achievements. His reign is most notable for the extensive building projects he commissioned, particularly in the Faiyum Oasis. Here, he undertook an ambitious irrigation project that significantly expanded the region's agricultural output, transforming it into one of Egypt's most fertile areas.

His architectural legacy is marked by the construction of the Labyrinth, an enormous and complex temple complex near the Hawara pyramid. This building was renowned in the ancient world for its size and complexity, consisting of thousands of rooms and chambers that amazed visitors. Amenemhat III also constructed two significant pyramids at Hawara and Dahshur, which are notable for their innovative design and construction techniques.

The Black Pyramid at Dahshur.
Tekisch, CC BY-SA 3.0 <https://creativecommons.org/licenses/by-sa/3.0>, via Wikimedia Commons; https://commons.wikimedia.org/wiki/File:Black_Pyramid_of_Amenemhat_III.JPG

Amenemhat III's reign was also characterized by stability and prosperity, which fostered advancements in literature, arts, and statecraft. His economic policies and construction projects provided employment and stimulated the economy, while his patronage of the arts led to a flourishing of cultural life.

In Summary

The Middle Kingdom was a period of significant achievements in various domains. These achievements not only revitalized Egyptian civilization but also set the stage for the subsequent New Kingdom. The invasion of a Middle Eastern group known as the Hyksos ended this remarkable period.

The New Kingdom (c. 1570-1069 BCE)

The New Kingdom, lasting from around the 16th century BCE to the 11th century BCE, represents one of the most illustrious chapters in ancient Egyptian history. This period, encompassing the Eighteenth, Nineteenth, and Twentieth Dynasties, is often regarded as the height of Egypt's power and cultural richness.

Politics

Egypt had been occupied by outsiders, the Hyksos, who were finally expelled from Egypt by Ahmose I. The return of the pharaoh's throne to Egypt laid the foundation for the New Kingdom.

One of the most significant aspects of the New Kingdom was its vast territorial expansion, making it the most powerful Egyptian empire. The era saw Egypt reaching its greatest extent, with its boundaries extending as far as the Euphrates River and Nubia under the reign of Thutmose III. This expansion was not merely an exercise of power but also a strategic defense mechanism against potential invasions, as experienced during the Second Intermediate Period.

Egypt in the 15ᵗʰ century BCE.
ArdadN, Jeff Dahl, CC BY-SA 3.0 <https://creativecommons.org/licenses/by-sa/3.0>, via Wikimedia Commons; https://commons.wikimedia.org/wiki/File:Egypt_NK_edit.svg

Thutmose III, often dubbed the "Napoleon of Egypt," consolidated Egypt's dominance in the Near East. Under his reign, Egypt asserted its authority over Syria, reorganized the military bureaucracy, and attained unprecedented levels of power and influence. This military expansion and consolidation under Thutmose III laid the foundations for Egypt's sustained regional dominance. His annals, recorded on the walls of the Karnak temple, are a primary source of information about these military exploits.[39]

A wealth of archaeological findings and historical texts provide evidence of Egypt's imperial aspirations. For instance, temples from this era, like those at Karnak and Luxor, are adorned with inscriptions and reliefs that provide valuable information. For example, the Battle of Kadesh is famously depicted in the reliefs found in the temples of Ramesses II, offering insights into his military campaigns.

The Valley of the Kings and the Valley of the Queens also offer a wealth of information for scholars to investigate. Tombs of pharaohs and high officials contain inscriptions, paintings, and artifacts that shed light on Egypt's foreign relations and military might.

Papyrus scrolls were not just records of military glory. Diplomatic relations were necessary for the empire's stability. Amenhotep III's reign, for example, was characterized by his use of marriage alliances to maintain peace and extend influence. Documents like the Amarna letters, which are a collection of diplomatic correspondence, reveal the political and diplomatic landscape of the New Kingdom and its relations with neighboring powers.[40]

Architecture and Art

The New Kingdom is renowned for its architectural marvels and artistic achievements. This period witnessed the construction of monumental structures like the temples at Karnak and Luxor, the Valley of the Kings, and the mortuary temple of Hatshepsut at Deir el-Bahri. These architectural feats showcased the Egyptians' advanced engineering and artistic skills and reflected their religious and cultural values.

Monumental temple complexes and elaborate tombs characterize the New Kingdom's architecture. Towering obelisks and colossal statues are testaments to the Egyptians' engineering prowess. New Kingdom pharaohs chose the Valley of the Kings as their final resting place, a shift reflecting both religious significance and concerns about tomb security. The valley was on the west bank of the Nile, where the sun set, so it had a symbolic relationship with death. The valley's isolation also offered better security from tomb robbers.

---

[39] Peter F. Dorman, M. S. (2024, January 19). Thutmose III. Retrieved from Britannica.com: https://www.britannica.com/biography/Thutmose-III/Adornment-of-Egypt.

[40] Scoville, P. (2015, November 6). Amarna Letters. Retrieved from Worldhistory.org: https://www.worldhistory.org/Amarna_Letters/.

The temples of Karnak and Luxor are the best examples of New Kingdom architecture. These complexes, with their colossal columns, expansive hypostyle halls, and intricate reliefs, were not only places of worship but also centers of economic activity. The expansion of the Karnak Temple Complex, particularly under Amenhotep III and Ramesses II, showcases the period's architectural ambition and religious devotion. The temple of Hatshepsut at Deir el-Bahri exemplifies the New Kingdom's architectural ingenuity. With its terraced design and harmonious integration into the surrounding cliffs, Hatshepsut's temple remains a masterpiece of ancient architecture.[41]

The temple of Hatshepsut.
Diego Delso, CC BY-SA 4.0 <https://creativecommons.org/licenses/by-sa/4.0>, via Wikimedia Commons; https://commons.wikimedia.org/wiki/File:Templo_funerario_de_Hatshepsut,_Luxor,_Egipto,_2022-01-03,_DD_13.jpg

The New Kingdom's architecture was imbued with deep symbolic and religious significance. Temples were often aligned with celestial bodies, reflecting the Egyptians' advanced understanding of astronomy and its integration into their religious and architectural concepts.

The grand building projects of the New Kingdom were not merely displays of religious and royal power but also significant drivers of the economy. They provided employment for many workers, artisans, and

---

[41] Pbs.org. (2024, January 19). Art & Architecture. Retrieved from Pbs.org: https://www.pbs.org/empires/egypt/newkingdom/architecture.html.

administrators and stimulated various sectors, such as agriculture, craft production, and transport. Politically, these architectural undertakings reinforced the pharaohs' divine status and legitimized their rule.[42]

Under Akhenaten, New Kingdom art experienced a significant shift, embracing what is known as the Amarna style. This period saw a move toward more naturalistic and less formal representations, especially in depictions of the royal family.

The New Kingdom also saw a proliferation of statues and sculptures ranging from colossal representations of pharaohs to smaller, more intimate statues of deities and individuals. These sculptures often display a high level of craftsmanship and realism. Items such as jewelry, pottery, and furniture found in tombs and archaeological sites are crucial in understanding the everyday artistic practices and aesthetic preferences of the New Kingdom. The skillful artistry seen in jewelry and decorative arts reflects a sophisticated understanding of materials and techniques.[43]

Economics

The New Kingdom witnessed economic prosperity fueled by wealth accumulated from military conquests, extensive trade networks, and efficient administrative systems. The Egyptians engaged in trade with their neighbors, exchanging gold, papyrus, linen, and grain for luxury items like incense, ivory, and exotic animals. This economic prosperity facilitated the construction of grand temples and tombs.

Control over trade routes and resources played a significant role in the New Kingdom's expansion. The wealth accumulated from these ventures funded military campaigns and building projects. Trade with regions like Punt, as depicted in the mortuary temple of Hatshepsut, is a testament to Egypt's economic outreach. The exchange of goods, ideas, and art during this period indicates a significant level of cultural interaction with other civilizations, such as the Nubians, Hittites, and Asiatic peoples.

---

[42] Brewminate.com. (2019, April 19). The Art and Architecture of New Kingdom Egypt c. 1570-1069.BCE. Retrieved from brewmintate.com: https://brewminate.com/the-art-and-architecture-of-new-kingdom-egypt-c-1570-1069-bce/.

[43] Pressbooks.bccampus.ca. (2024, January 19). New Kingdom Art. Retrieved from pressbooks.bccampus.ca: https://pressbooks.bccampus.ca/cavestocathedrals/chapter/new-kingdom/.

Religious Upheaval

The New Kingdom was also a time of significant religious transformation. The most notable was the religious revolution under Akhenaten, who established monotheism centered around the worship of Aten, the sun disk. He moved the capital to Akhetaten (modern-day Amarna) and promoted Aten as the supreme deity, diminishing the traditional polytheistic belief system. Although this shift was short-lived, it had a profound impact on Egyptian religion.

The shift to monotheism, or more precisely monolatrism (the worship of one god without denying the existence of others), was unprecedented in Egyptian history. Akhenaten's religious reform involved the elevation of Aten and the systematic diminution of other gods, most notably Amun.

The religious reforms of Akhenaten had significant sociopolitical implications. By diminishing the role of other deities, Akhenaten sought to reduce the power and wealth of the priesthood. This move can be interpreted as an attempt to centralize religious and political authority under the pharaoh.

Following Akhenaten's death, there was a rapid restoration of the traditional polytheistic religious practices. His successor, Tutankhamun (the famous King Tut), played a pivotal role in this religious restoration. The capital was moved back to Thebes, and efforts were made to erase the changes, including the destruction or defacement of Akhenaten's monuments. This swift reversal highlights the deep-seated nature of traditional religious beliefs and practices in ancient Egyptian society.

Akhenaten's reign witnessed profound changes in artistic styles. Traditional rigid and formal artistic norms gave way to more naturalistic and relaxed forms, particularly in the portrayal of the royal family. This new art style, characterized by elongated faces and bodies, was a reflection of the broader religious and cultural shifts of the time.[44]

The Impactful Pharaohs

Some of Egypt's most legendary rulers graced the New Kingdom. Ahmose I, considered the founder of the Eighteenth Dynasty, successfully drove out the Hyksos invaders and unified Egypt. His

---

[44] Taronas, L. (2024, January 19). Akhenaten: The Mysteries of Religious Revolution. Retrieved from Arce.org: https://arce.org/resource/akhenaten-mysteries-religious-revolution/.

successors, including Amenhotep I, Thutmose I, and Amenhotep III, continued to fortify and expand the empire.

A defining feature of this era was the remarkable reign of Queen Hatshepsut, one of the most influential and successful female monarchs in history. Hatshepsut, known for her effective administration and ambitious building projects, significantly contributed to Egypt's prosperity and architectural grandeur.

- Ahmose I (c. 1549-1524 BCE)

    The founder of the Eighteenth Dynasty, Ahmose I was the architect of the New Kingdom. His significance lies in his successful campaigns against the Hyksos, the foreign rulers who had occupied northern Egypt. By expelling them, Ahmose unified Egypt. His military achievements laid the groundwork for the prosperity and power that Egypt would enjoy in the centuries to come.

- Hatshepsut (c. 1479-1458 BCE)

    Hatshepsut, one of the few female pharaohs in ancient Egyptian history, was a figure of profound importance. Her reign was one of peace and economic growth. Hatshepsut is best known for her ambitious building projects, most notably the temple at Deir el-Bahri. Her successful trading expedition to Punt brought wealth and exotic goods and animals to Egypt, enhancing its cultural and economic status.

- Thutmose III (c. 1479-1425 BCE)

    Thutmose III, the stepson of Hatshepsut, emerged as one of the greatest pharaohs of the New Kingdom. His military campaigns expanded Egypt's borders to their furthest extent, extending Egyptian influence into Asia and Nubia. His reign was not just about conquest; he also significantly contributed to the arts and architecture in Egypt, commissioning numerous temples and monuments.

- Amenhotep III (c. 1386-1349 BCE)

    Amenhotep III's reign was marked by peace, prosperity, and artistic flourishing. Known for his diplomatic skills, he maintained Egypt's position through strategic marriages and alliances rather than military might. His architectural contributions are monumental, including significant additions to the Karnak Temple Complex and the construction of the Colossi of Memnon. His reign is often seen as the height of Egyptian artistic and cultural sophistication.

The Colossi of Memnon in 2015.
MusikAnimal, CC BY-SA 4.0 <https://creativecommons.org/licenses/by-sa/4.0>, via Wikimedia Commons; https://commons.wikimedia.org/wiki/File:Colossi_of_Memnon_May_2015_2.JPG

- Akhenaten (Amenhotep IV) (c. 1353-1336 BCE)

    Akhenaten, originally Amenhotep IV, is remembered for his religious revolution. He replaced Egypt's traditional polytheistic religion with the worship of a single god, Aten, and moved the capital to Akhetaten. His reign brought about a distinctive artistic style that emphasized realism. Although his religious reforms were controversial and largely reversed after his death, they represented a significant departure from traditional Egyptian culture and religion.

- King Tutankhamun (c. 1333-1323 BCE)

    The boy king of Egypt's reign saw the restoration of the old religious practices. Besides that, there is nothing really noteworthy about his reign besides his mysterious death at a young age. His tomb discovery was a major archaeological event because it was untouched by robbers. Before this discovery, we could only imagine how amazing the tombs of rulers were before they were robbed.

- Ramesses II (c. 1279-1213 BCE)

    Ramesses II, also known as Ramesses the Great, was one of the longest-reigning pharaohs of the New Kingdom. His reign was marked by architectural brilliance, military campaigns, and a large family that ensured a succession of rulers from his lineage. He is best known for the Battle of Kadesh against the Hittites, which led to the signing of the first recorded peace treaty in history. His building projects, including the construction of the magnificent Abu Simbel temples and the Ramesseum, his funerary temple, are among the most impressive in Egyptian history.

These pharaohs of the New Kingdom left an indelible mark on Egyptian history. Each ruler, in their unique way, contributed to the empire's prosperity and cultural richness. Their legacies have stood the test of time, from military conquests and religious reforms to architectural wonders and artistic achievements. Under their leadership, the New Kingdom witnessed the peak of Egyptian civilization.

The End of the New Kingdom

Despite its grandeur, the New Kingdom eventually succumbed to internal strife and external pressures, leading to its decline. The power struggle between the pharaohs and the high priests of Amun, coupled with the rise of regional rulers, weakened central authority. The New Kingdom's end marked the beginning of a period of fragmentation and foreign domination.

Nevertheless, the legacy of the New Kingdom is enduring. The architectural and artistic achievements of this period continue to captivate the world. Moreover, the New Kingdom's influence extended beyond its borders, impacting neighboring cultures and later civilizations.

The Ptolemaic Era (323-30 BCE)

Egypt's decline after the end of the New Kingdom included being conquered by outsiders, including the Kushites (who founded the Twenty-fifth Dynasty), the Assyrians, and the Persians. A significant change occurred in the 4th century BCE when Alexander the Great seized Egypt and ushered in the Ptolemaic era.

The Ptolemaic era stands out as a remarkable period in ancient history. It was a time marked by profound cultural, economic, political, and religious accomplishments, significantly shaping Egypt's historical narrative. Politically, the Ptolemaic era was characterized by relative stability and effective governance. The Ptolemies, adopting the title of pharaoh, skillfully integrated themselves into Egyptian society. By participating in Egyptian religious practices and respecting traditional customs, they gained acceptance and legitimacy among the Egyptian people. This approach to governance helped maintain internal stability and fostered a sense of unity within the kingdom.[45]

A remarkable aspect of the Ptolemaic era was the synthesis of Greek and Egyptian cultures. This fusion is evident in various forms of artistic expression, such as sculpture, where Greek hairstyles and features were combined with traditional Egyptian attributes. This cultural blend was not just a creative endeavor but also a strategic move to create a harmonious society, amalgamating the traditions of the Greek rulers with those of the Egyptian populace.

The Ptolemaic rulers were adept at expanding their territory and influence. Ptolemy II successfully grew the size of Egypt. These expansions were not military conquests and shrewd diplomatic maneuvers, such as establishing trade posts along the Red Sea and engaging in marriages for alliance-building. Such policies helped solidify Egypt's position in the region and enhanced its influence in the Mediterranean world.[46]

The Library of Alexandria

The Library of Alexandria was the premier accomplishment of the Ptolemaic era. This institution was not just a repository of books; it was also the epicenter of learning and intellectual activity in the ancient world. It was part of a scholarly complex known as the Mouseion that the Ptolemies constructed to advance knowledge and the study of ideas. Scholars from various disciplines gathered here, contributing to an unprecedented exchange of ideas and expertise. The library's comprehensive collection of manuscripts made it a beacon of scholarship and education.[47]

---

[45] New World Encyclopedia. (2024, January 19). Ptolemaic Dynasty. Retrieved from New World Encyclopedia: https://www.newworldencyclopedia.org/entry/Ptolemaic_dynasty.

[46] Wasson, D. L. (2016, September 29). Ptolemaic Dynasty. Retrieved from Worldhistory.org: https://www.worldhistory.org/Ptolemaic_Dynasty/.

[47] Haughton, B. (2011, February 1). What Happened to the Great Library at Alexandria? Retrieved from Worldhistory.org: https://www.worldhistory.org/article/207/what-happened-to-the-great-library-at-alexandria/.

The library was built by Ptolemy II Philadelphus, who purchased the library's first books. Succeeding pharaohs continued buying manuscripts but devised a novel way of expanding the library's collection. Books were taken from ships entering the harbor of Alexandria and copied, with the originals then becoming the library's property.[48]

The Library of Alexandria's collection was staggering in volume and diversity. Estimates suggest it held over half a million scrolls, encompassing a vast array of subjects from epic poetry and drama to science and religion.

Scholars resided in Alexandria, enjoying royal patronage that allowed them to focus exclusively on their studies and teachings. Among them were Euclid, Herophilus, and Archimedes, whose works profoundly influenced subsequent generations.

The Library of Alexandria remains a subject of fascination and study, symbolizing the zenith of ancient scholarship and the tragic loss of cultural and intellectual heritage. In modern times, the revival of the Bibliotheca Alexandrina aims to recapture the spirit of its ancient namesake. Inaugurated in 2002, this modern library and cultural center in Alexandria seeks to rekindle the old library's legacy of learning and dialogue. This institution stands as a testament to the enduring allure of the Library of Alexandria and its lasting impact on the collective imagination of humankind.

Economy

Agriculture saw substantial advancements under Ptolemaic rule. The rulers implemented effective land reclamation and irrigation strategies, significantly increasing the cultivable land area. Introducing new crops, such as olives and superior wine-producing grapes, further diversified and enriched the agricultural sector. These innovations not only boosted the economy but also improved the quality of life for the Egyptian populace.[49]

The Ptolemaic era marked a significant transition in Egypt's economy with the introduction of a minted currency system. This shift from a barter to a monetized economy facilitated trade and commerce

---

[48] Mark, J. J. (2023, July 25). Library of Alexandria. Retrieved from Worldhistory.org: https://www.worldhistory.org/Library_of_Alexandria/.

[49] Ancientegptianfacts.com. (2024, January 19). Facts About Ancient Egyptians. Retrieved from Ancientegptianfacts.com: https://ancientegyptianfacts.com/ptolemaic-period-egypt.html.

domestically and internationally. The Ptolemies established Egypt as a pivotal trade corridor, linking the Mediterranean with Africa and the Indian Ocean. This enhanced Egypt's position as an economic powerhouse in the ancient world.[50]

The Harbor and the Pharos

The harbor of Alexandria was the epicenter of Ptolemaic Egypt's prosperity. As the busiest trading center in the Mediterranean, the harbor of Alexandria was instrumental in facilitating the growth and prosperity of Alexandria, making it the largest city of the ancient world at that time. The harbor's design and management were integral to its success as a commercial hub. Greek architects meticulously planned the city on a grid pattern, complete with wide main streets and framed by the significant Gates of the Sun and the Moon.[51]

Amidst Alexandria's architectural marvels, the Lighthouse of Alexandria, also known as the Pharos of Alexandria, stood as a testament to the city's advanced engineering and architectural capabilities. Constructed during the reigns of Ptolemy I and Ptolemy II, this monumental structure was one of the Seven Wonders of the Ancient World. Towering over one hundred meters tall, the Pharos was not just an impressive edifice but also a beacon of safety and guidance for sailors navigating the treacherous waters of the Mediterranean.

Its primary function was to guide ships safely into Alexandria's harbor. Historians believe that a fire, likely fueled by oil due to the scarcity of wood, was kept burning at the top of the tower to ensure visibility at night. This feature was groundbreaking for its time, and the Pharos soon became a model for lighthouses throughout the ancient world. The lighthouse's design possibly included a polished bronze mirror, reflecting the flame over greater distances and functioning as a sunlight reflector during the day.[52]

---

[50] King, A. (2018, July 25). The Economy of Ptolemaic Egypt. Retrieved from Worldhistory.org: https://www.worldhistory.org/article/1256/the-economy-of-ptolemaic-egypt/.

[51] Bevan, E. (2024, January 19). Chapter IV: The People, the Cities, the Court. Retrieved from Penelope.uchicago.edu: https://penelope.uchicago.edu/Thayer/E/Gazetteer/Places/Africa/Egypt/_Texts/BEVHOP/4B*.html.

[52] Cartwright, M. (2018, July 24). Lighthouse of Alexandria. Retrieved from Worldhistory.org: https://www.worldhistory.org/Lighthouse_of_Alexandria/.

Prominent Pharaohs of Ptolemaic Egypt
- Ptolemy I Soter (323-282 BCE)

  Ptolemy I Soter, a general under Alexander the Great, assumed control of Egypt after Alexander's demise in 323 BCE and founded the Ptolemaic dynasty. His reign laid the foundations for the Hellenistic culture in Egypt. Ptolemy I's most notable achievement was the urban development of Alexandria, which would become a flourishing hub of commerce and Hellenistic culture. Under his rule, Alexandria emerged as a beacon of learning and culture, attracting scholars and artists from across the Mediterranean world.

- Ptolemy II Philadelphus (285-246 BCE)

  Ptolemy II Philadelphus, the son of Ptolemy I, is renowned for his cultural and economic contributions. He significantly expanded the Library of Alexandria, making it a symbol of scholarly excellence and a repository of vast knowledge. Under his reign, Alexandria witnessed unparalleled cultural growth, becoming the epitome of Hellenistic sophistication. Ptolemy II also focused on strengthening Egypt's economy. He established extensive trade networks and improved agricultural practices, ensuring prosperity and stability in the kingdom.

- Ptolemy III Euergetes (246-222 BCE)

  Ptolemy III Euergetes inherited a stable and prosperous kingdom. He is remembered for his military prowess and expansionist policies. His reign was marked by the successful Third Syrian War, which expanded Egypt's territorial boundaries. Ptolemy III's military campaigns were not only about land acquisition; they also served to secure trade routes and resources, bolstering Egypt's economic and strategic position in the region. His rule was also a period of cultural and economic flourishing, continuing the legacy of his predecessors in supporting the arts, sciences, and economic development.

- Cleopatra VII Philopator (51-30 BCE)

  Cleopatra VII, arguably the most famous of the Ptolemaic rulers, was a figure renowned for her intelligence, political savvy, and charisma. Her reign was marked by tumultuous events and strategic alliances with key Roman figures like Julius Caesar and Mark Antony. Cleopatra's primary goal was to preserve Egypt's independence amid the rising star of Rome. She undertook extensive efforts to revitalize Egypt's economy and restore its former glory. However, her reign culminated in tragedy with her defeat at the Battle of Actium and subsequent suicide, leading to the fall of the Ptolemaic dynasty and Egypt's annexation by Rome.

Cleopatra's legacy is complex; she is remembered for her attempts to revive Egypt's fortunes and for her role in the dynasty's eventual downfall.

The Ptolemaic era ended with the death of Cleopatra and Egypt's absorption into the Roman Republic. Egypt would continue to be an economic power in the Mediterranean, but it would be a subjected nation. Egypt's glory days were over, at least for the moment.

The Ptolemaic dynasty was a time of intrigue, power, cultural fusion, and dramatic shifts in the political landscape of the ancient world. Egypt navigated an epoch that saw complex political scenarios and economic growth while nurturing a cultural environment that was unparalleled for its time. Ancient Egypt is an amazing saga in the history of humanity.

Chapter 7: Kerma

The Kingdom of Kerma was the earliest known centralized state in the Nile Valley south of Egypt. It was located at the site of the modern city of Kerma in northern Sudan. Kerma's society was characterized by a sophisticated culture with distinctive pottery, architecture, and a system of governance. Kerma was the middleman between Egypt and the African interior. The Kingdom of Kerma eventually succumbed to the expansion of the New Kingdom of Egypt under Thutmose I, and it was incorporated into the Egyptian empire.

<u>Interesting Political Structure</u>

A challenge scholars have with the Kerma civilization is that Kerma did not have a written alphabet, so what we know about this kingdom comes from Egyptian sources. This, of course, means Kerma's recorded history is biased in favor of the Egyptians. We do know that after Kerma absorbed the Sai Island Kingdom, the new state rivaled Egypt in size. The Kingdom of Kerma extended north to the First Cataract of the Nile River. We also know that Kerma was not a primitive assortment of tribes but had a social structure and governance that equaled Egypt.

Women had a role in ruling Kerma and would be co-rulers with their husbands or reign alone as sovereign queens. Provinces within the Kingdom of Kerma played a crucial role in its administrative machinery. Each province was managed by a governor known as a *pesto*, ensuring the smooth functioning of their respective provinces. They had a cadre of subordinates under them, indicating Kerma had a structured bureaucratic system.

These monarchs were not only political leaders but also held religious significance, predominantly worshiping Amun, a deity shared with Egyptian religious traditions. This centralized religious practice underlined the kingdom's governance and cultural identity.

The military strength of Kerma was a testament to its effective governance. Known as "the Land of the Bow," Kerma's soldiers were renowned for their archery skills. In addition, the Kermite warriors used spears, pikes, and khopesh swords. Their military might protected the kingdom from external threats and played a role in its expansionist policies.[53]

The social organization in Kerma, as evidenced by its burial practices, revealed a society where wealth and status extended beyond the ruling class. The cemeteries feature elaborate tombs for the ruling elite, prosperous merchants, and other affluent individuals, suggesting a nuanced social stratification within the kingdom.

Excavations at Kerma.
Lassi, CC BY-SA 4.0 <https://creativecommons.org/licenses/by-sa/4.0>, via Wikimedia Commons; https://commons.wikimedia.org/wiki/File:Kerma_city.JPG

---

[53] Team, E. (2018, November 3). The Kingdom of Kerma (2500-1500 BC). Retrieved from Thinkafrica.net: https://thinkafrica.net/the-kingdom-of-kerma-2500-1500-bc/.

The Economy of Kerma

The kingdom's strategic location on trade routes from central Africa to the Mediterranean allowed its economy to thrive. Kerma's rulers capitalized on their lucrative position by imposing taxes and tolls on trade caravans passing through their territory, contributing significantly to the kingdom's wealth.

Kerma's economy was bolstered by its rich natural resources, including gold, cattle, dairy products, ebony, ivory, and other valuable materials. Exploiting these resources under a centralized governance system facilitated economic prosperity, a key element in sustaining the kingdom's power and influence. Kerma excelled in industries such as metalworking and pottery.

Ancient Kerma bowl.
https://commons.wikimedia.org/wiki/File:Wallpaper_group-pmg-1.jpg

A Deal with the Devil

Kerma's relationship with ancient Egypt was multifaceted, encompassing both cooperative and antagonistic elements. During the Middle Kerma Period(c. 1990-1725 BCE), which coincided with the Middle Kingdom of Egypt, there was Egyptian military activity in Lower

Nubia that suggests that Kerma was perceived as a significant threat to Egyptian interests. This era saw the construction of major Egyptian fortifications in the Middle Nile Valley, aimed at protecting the Upper Egyptian border against Kerma raids and securing valuable trade routes. The resources that Kerma possessed were highly coveted by Egypt, further fueling the rivalry.

Kerma ordinarily prospered when Egypt was in decline. The Hyksos' seizure of Lower Egypt gave Kerma a chance to gain a considerable regional advantage. The alliance between Kerma and the Hyksos during the Egyptian-Hyksos conflict is a fascinating example of ancient geopolitical maneuvering that influenced the relationships between states.[54]

The Hyksos were a group of Asiatic peoples who established themselves in Lower Egypt. The Second Intermediate Period of Egypt was a time of political fragmentation, and the Hyksos capitalized on Egypt's vulnerability by taking control of the northeastern Nile Delta and forming a significant military and political force in the region.

Previous Egyptian military actions likely influenced Kerma's decision to align with the Hyksos in the region. Kerma might have viewed an alliance with the Hyksos as a strategic move to counterbalance Egyptian power and protect its economic interests. A period of Egyptian internal weakness was an opportunity for Kerma to expand its power. This partnership allowed Kerma to extend its borders into Egypt and attack southern Egypt.

Caught between the Hyksos and Kerma, Egypt was helpless. However, this state of affairs did not last for long.[55]

Kerma's invasion and looting of Egyptian treasures was a humiliation Egypt would not forget. The Egyptian pharaohs of the Seventeenth Dynasty (c. 1580-1550 BCE) waged military campaigns against the Hyksos, who were being supported by Kermite mercenaries. Ahmose I, the founder of Egypt's Eighteenth Dynasty, defeated the Hyksos, ending their period of power. Kerma now became the target of Egyptian

---

[54] DeMola, P. (2013, March 14). Interrelations of Kerma and Pharaonic Egypt. Retrieved from World History Encyclopedia: https://www.worldhistory.org/article/487/interrelations-of-kerma-and-pharaonic-egypt/.

[55] Team, E. (2018, November 3). The Kingdom of Kerma (2500-1500 BC). Retrieved from Thinkafrica.net: https://thinkafrica.net/the-kingdom-of-kerma-2500-1500-bc/.

revenge.

After the Egyptians expelled the Hyksos, they launched punitive campaigns against Kerma, particularly during the reign of Pharaoh Thutmose I. The primary objectives of the Egyptian invasion were to neutralize the threat posed by Kerma, reassert Egyptian control over Nubia, and directly access the region's rich gold resources. Thutmose I's military campaign against Kerma was a calculated effort to remove a growing danger and to reclaim lost territories and resources.

Thutmose I pushed southward into Nubia. The Egyptian army, known for its chariots and archers, advanced toward Kerma's capital, overcoming its defenses. These campaigns culminated in a decisive Egyptian victory in 1504 BCE and the subsequent annexation of the Kingdom of Kerma into the Egyptian empire.

Egyptianization of Kerman

The conquest of Kerma had significant cultural and political consequences. The annexation led to the Egyptianization of the region, with Kerma's unique cultural identity increasingly influenced by Egyptian culture. This included adopting Egyptian religious practices, art forms, and administrative systems. Despite this cultural integration, there were continued instances of rebellion and resistance in the region, but these did not change the fate of the Nubian kingdom. Kerma became a significant province of the Egyptian empire economically, politically, and spiritually.[56]

In Summary

The Kingdom of Kerma stands out as a remarkable example of effective governance and sophisticated provincial administration in the ancient world. Its centralized political structure, efficient local governance, economic prosperity, military strength, and advanced urban planning collectively underscored a civilization that was both complex and progressive for its time.

---

[56] DeMola, P. (2013, March 14). Interrelations of Kerma and Pharaonic Egypt. Retrieved from World History Encyclopedia: https://www.worldhistory.org/article/487/interrelations-of-kerma-and-pharaonic-egypt/.

Chapter 8: Ancient Carthage

We often think of empires as vast expanses of land exploited for their natural resources that are forcibly extracted or cut from the ground. This image includes large occupational garrisons. However, some ancient empires did not consist of expansive provinces; instead, they had extensive coastal outposts. Those imperial nations relied on trade and did not always extend deep into the interior.

Carthage was an ancient empire whose holdings were based on commercial opportunity. Carthage was a maritime power that emphasized trade over other imperial concerns. It had nearly total control over the sea lanes in the western Mediterranean.

Roots in the Middle East

Virgil's *Aeneid* spins a tale of how Queen Dido founded Carthage. She supposedly laid out thin strips of ox hide in a semicircle around a hill with the sea forming one side. It is a delightful legend, but this story of the city's founding is pure fiction. The real story of Carthage began in what is now Lebanon; the main characters were the Phoenicians.

The Phoenicians established several colonies across the Mediterranean to facilitate their extensive trade network. Carthage, located on the coast of modern-day Tunisia, was one of these colonies. The city's Phoenician name, Qart Hadasht, meaning "New City," reflected its status as a new venture by these enterprising seafarers. Modern historians and archaeologists have examined both Carthaginian and external records and have largely settled on 814 BCE as the most probable date for Carthage's founding. This is based on a convergence of historical documents and archaeological data despite earlier foundation dates suggested by some ancient sources.

The strategic location of Carthage was crucial to its success. Positioned on the Tunisian coast, it controlled the passage between Sicily and the North African coast, making it an ideal spot for a thriving port and trading center. This advantageous position allowed Carthage to dominate maritime trade routes across the western Mediterranean.[57]

Initially a colony of Tyre, Carthage gradually asserted its independence, especially after Tyre fell to the Babylonians in 573 BCE. Carthage started to establish its colonies and expand its territory in Africa, marking the beginning of its transformation into a mighty empire.[58]

Ties to the Motherland

Carthage retained a strong Phoenician (Punic) identity despite its political independence. The Punic language, a dialect of Phoenician, was spoken in Carthage and remained in use for centuries after the city's fall. This retention of language and cultural practices illustrates the enduring influence of Phoenician culture in Carthage.

Government

Initially, Carthage likely operated under a monarchical system akin to other Phoenician city-states. The kings, while pivotal, did not exercise absolute power and worked alongside a council of advisors known as the Adirim, comprised of wealthy and influential members of society. This council played a crucial role in important state matters, including religion, administration, and military affairs. The Carthaginian senate (known as the *drm*) was a body of influential citizens who served for life,

A significant shift occurred in Carthaginian governance around 480 BCE after the death of King Hamilcar I. This period marked the gradual weakening of the monarchy and the rise of an oligarchic republic characterized by a complex administrative system, checks and balances, and public accountability.

---

[57] Hunt, P. (2024, January 22). Carthage. Retrieved from Britannica.com: https://www.britannica.com/place/Carthage-ancient-city-Tunisia.

[58] Dickinson College Commentaries. (2024, January 22). Carthage: Early History. Retrieved from dcc.dickoinson.edu: https://dcc.dickinson.edu/nepos-hannibal/carthage-early-history.

The Suffetes

At the top of the Carthaginian government were two suffetes, akin to modern-day presidents or prime ministers. They were annually elected by the city's wealthiest and most influential families. Contrary to the absolute monarchies of the time, the suffetes had limited terms and wielded judicial and executive powers. Their roles involved convening the supreme council, submitting issues to the popular assembly, and overseeing trials. This system indicated a plutocratic society where wealth played a crucial role in political participation.

Gerousia and the Magistrates of Five

Aristotle commented on Carthage's constitution and paid particular attention to the Gerousia, a council of elders. Comprising twenty-eight members chosen for life, this council advised magistrates and generals, oversaw justice administration, and served as an appellate court. Its members, selected from distinguished families, were typically over sixty years old, reflecting a system that revered experience and wisdom.

The Magistrates of Five, another essential body in Carthaginian politics, were responsible for justice and finances. Chosen for one-year terms, they played a significant role in the city's governance, particularly in selecting the Supreme Council of One Hundred. Over time, their influence waned, but their early role underscores the complexity of Carthaginian governance.

Aristotle believed Carthage's constitution was more oligarchic than aristocratic, as significant power was concentrated in the hands of a wealthy few. This oligarchy was maintained through a system that enriched sections of the populace, thereby stabilizing the state. The rulers, often wealthy individuals, were chosen not just for their merit but also for their financial status, reflecting a society where economic power translated into political influence.[59]

A distinctive feature of Carthaginian governance was its judicial board of 104 members, which examined the actions of military generals and other officials. This body, comprising lifelong senators, was tasked with assessing military commanders' performance and holding them accountable for the outcomes of their campaigns. A general who lost

---

[59] EDU, W. H. (2023, May 10). Aristotle's Analysis of the Carthaginian Constitution. Retrieved from Worldhistory.edu: https://worldhistoryedu.com/aristotles-analysis-of-the-carthaginian-constitution/.

could expect harsh consequences. Substantial fines might be imposed, and, in extreme cases, crucifixion could be the sentence. The range of penalties for failed campaigns underscores the stringent standards upheld by Carthage. Suicide was a means of avoiding execution.

The administrative structure of the Carthaginian Empire was marked by a degree of autonomy for regional governors, particularly in local governance, while retaining centralized control in military and foreign affairs. This balance of local autonomy and central oversight was crucial for managing Carthage's expansive territories, which spanned parts of North Africa, the Iberian Peninsula, and various Mediterranean islands. While enjoying a measure of self-rule, these regions were obligated to pay tribute and provide military support to Carthage.[60]

Society

Carthage had a popular assembly known as the 'm (ham), which was responsible for voting on issues proposed by the suffetes and senate and for electing officials, including the suffetes, chief priest, treasurer, and military commanders.

Carthaginian citizenship was male-dominated. Women, slaves, and foreigners were not allowed to participate in government. One's social and political life in Carthage was primarily determined by one's status as a citizen, artisan, foreigner, or slave. Artisans, less skilled workers, women, and slaves formed a significant portion of the city's population and contributed to its economic prosperity.[61]

The religious landscape of Carthage, rooted in Phoenician polytheism, significantly influenced its cultural and political life. The empire's artisans and traders dealt in a wide array of commodities, including spices, textiles, and slaves, demonstrating Carthage's economic diversity and its pivotal role in ancient trade networks.[62]

---

[60] Cartwright, M. (2016, June 16). Carthaginian Society. Retrieved from Worldhistory.org: https://www.worldhistory.org/article/908/carthaginian-society/.

[61] Cartwright, M. (2016, June 16). Carthaginian Society. Retrieved from Worldhistory.org: https://www.worldhistory.org/article/908/carthaginian-society/.

[62] LibreTexts. (2024, January 22). 4.2 Ancient Carthage. Retrieved from Libretexts.org: https://human.libretexts.org/Courses/Lumen_Learning/Book%3A_Early_World_Civilizations_(Lumen)/Ch._03_Early_Civilizations_of_Africa_and_the_Andes/04.2%3A_Ancient_Carthage.

The Economy

Economically, Carthage was a powerhouse. Carthage's economy was predominantly driven by its extensive trade network, which spanned from the western Mediterranean to the shores of North Africa and beyond. The city-state's strategic location near the narrow sea passage between Sicily and North Africa placed it at the crossroads of vital maritime routes, facilitating the flow of goods in the Mediterranean. Carthage's harbors buzzed with ships loaded with a variety of goods, highlighting the city's central role in Mediterranean commerce.

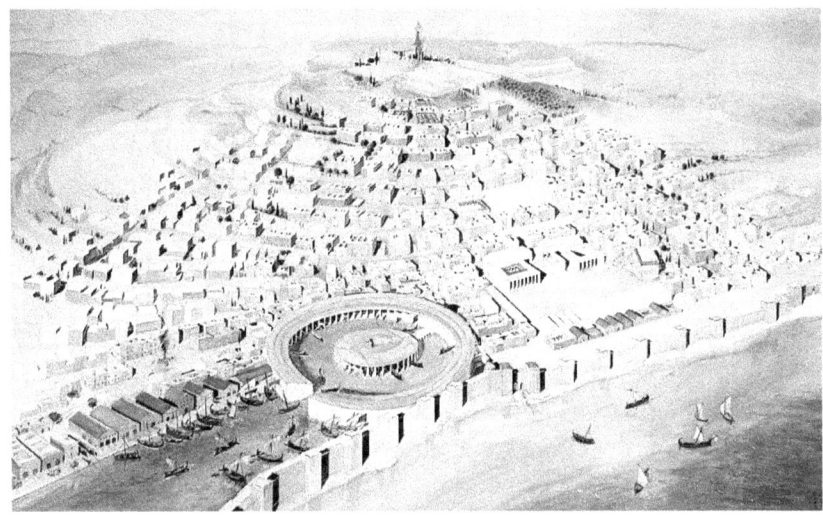

A modern illustration of what Carthage once looked like.
damian entwistle, CC BY-SA 2.0 <https://creativecommons.org/licenses/by-sa/2.0>, via Wikimedia Commons;
https://commons.wikimedia.org/wiki/File:Carthage_National_Museum_representation_of_city.jpg

The spirit of exploration was evident in Carthaginian society, as exemplified by navigators like Hanno and Himilco. Their voyages extended Carthage's influence and opened new trade routes. Hanno's exploration along the African coast and Himilco's ventures along the northwestern shores of Europe were not just about discovery but also about establishing new trade connections and colonies.[63]

Carthage was renowned for its diverse trade, dealing in precious metals like gold, silver, tin, and copper alongside everyday commodities

---

[63] Staff, E. (2021, October 31). Carthaginian Trade: Trade Routes of Ancient Carthage. Retrieved from Carthagemagazine.com: https://carthagemagazine.com/carthaginian-trade-routes-of-ancient-carthage/.

like animal skins, wool, and ivory. A significant and darker aspect of their trade was in slaves. The city was also known for its craftsmanship, producing and exporting art, textiles, weapons, and a range of manufactured goods. The Carthaginian navy, a powerful force in the Mediterranean, protected these trade interests and aggressively maintained control over critical maritime routes.[64]

Carthaginian Military

The Carthaginian Empire, known for its formidable presence in the ancient Mediterranean world, presents a picture of military might and sophisticated governance. Following substantial losses in the Sicilian Wars during the 5th and 4th centuries BCE, Carthage resorted to an extraordinary military strategy: the extensive use of mercenary forces.

This pivot was necessitated by the need to replenish their depleted ranks. Carthaginian recruiters scoured the Mediterranean, drawing soldiers from diverse regions, including Gaul, Iberia, Libya, and Greece.

A distinct feature of the Carthaginian military was its use of war elephants and chariots. These elephants, often armored, were deployed to disrupt enemy formations. Despite their formidable presence on the battlefield, their effectiveness was tempered by their unpredictability and the enemy's adaptation strategies. Chariots, used until the 3rd century BCE, were primarily operational in North Africa and southern Spain, highlighting Carthage's adaptation of its military tactics to different terrains.

A blend of heavy infantry formations akin to the Greek phalanx and agile cavalry and skirmishers characterized Carthaginian military strategies. However, the effectiveness of these forces hinged significantly on the commander's ability to galvanize such a varied contingent into a unified, formidable force.[65]

---

[64] Cartwright, M. (2016, June 17). Carthaginian Trade. Retrieved from Worldhistory.org: https://www.worldhistory.org/article/911/carthaginian-trade/.

[65] Cartwright, M. (2916, January 8). Carthaginian Army. Retrieved from Worldhistory.org: https://www.worldhistory.org/Carthaginian_Army/.

The Punic Wars
First Punic War (264-241 BCE)

The western Mediterranean just before the start of the First Punic War.
Harrias, CC BY-SA 4.0 <https://creativecommons.org/licenses/by-sa/4.0>, via Wikimedia Commons; https://commons.wikimedia.org/wiki/File:First_Punic_War_264_BC_v3.png

Carthage was the uncontested power in the western Mediterranean for centuries, but by 300 BCE, that status was beginning to change. The Roman Republic had grown from a small cluster of settlements to become the primary power in the Italian Peninsula. And it was expanding. It would not be long before Carthage and Rome would lock horns.

The First Punic War, a significant and lengthy conflict fought between Rome and Carthage, offers a fascinating study of the interplay of military innovation, economic resources, and strategic diplomacy. Fought primarily for the control of Sicily, the war reshaped the power dynamics in the Mediterranean and laid the groundwork for future Roman expansion.

The Conflict's Origins

The genesis of the First Punic War can be traced to the complicated geopolitical situation in Sicily. The island was a melting pot of cultures and various powers. The Greeks, Carthaginians, and native Sicilian tribes often fought for supremacy. Sicily's strategic location in the center of the Mediterranean made it a valuable naval base and commercial asset. The immediate cause of the war was a conflict involving Messana, a city in Sicily.

The Mamertines, mercenaries of Italian origin, had seized control of the city and faced opposition from King Hieron II of Syracuse. Their appeal for help turned into a diplomatic crisis when both Rome and Carthage responded, thus setting the stage for a broader conflict.[66]

The naval engagements defined the war. Rome went from being a land power to having one of the most powerful navies in the ancient world. Carthage had a long-standing tradition of seafaring and thus had a powerful navy. Rome initially could not stand up to its maritime enemy. However, the Romans demonstrated exceptional adaptability and resourcefulness and embarked on a rapid naval buildup.

They introduced the corvus, a boarding bridge that allowed them to leverage their superior infantry tactics at sea. This innovation was pivotal in their first significant naval victory at the Battle of Mylae in 260 BCE and later at the major Battle of Ecnomus in 256 BCE. While not decisively ending Carthaginian naval dominance, these victories showcased Roman tenacity and ingenuity.

Rome was not the only military innovator. Carthage enlisted the Spartan captain Xanthippus to reorganize its army. Embracing the Macedonian model of combined arms, Xanthippus restructured the army to maximize the effectiveness of its diverse elements, including its cavalry, elephants, and a citizen phalanx.

The Romans under Marcus Atilius invaded North Africa in 256 BCE. The Romans initially enjoyed success, but Xanthippus eventually defeated them. His military reforms resulted in a major victory at the Battle of Bagradas River in 255 BC, where the reformed Carthaginian forces decisively defeated the Romans.[67]

Despite this setback, Rome's determination did not waver. The Romans continued to rebuild their fleet, even after suffering tremendous losses due to storms and battles. The Roman Senate mobilized financial resources and manpower, often through private contributions, and demonstrated a firm commitment to the strategic goals of Rome.

Conversely, Carthage faced several strategic and resource challenges. The Carthaginians' inability to effectively capitalize on their initial naval supremacy was a critical factor. The war significantly strained

---

[66] Editors, H. (2013, June 12). Punic Wars. Retrieved from Hisory.com: https://www.history.com/topics/ancient-rome/punic-wars#first-punic-war-264-241-b-c.

[67] Lynch, P. (201, May 5). A Brutal and Bloody Affair: 6 Key Battles That Decided the First Punic War. Retrieved from Historycollection.com: https://historycollection.com/roman-military-might-6-key-battles-decided-first-punic-war/.

Carthaginian finances and military resources, leading them to seek aid, such as from Ptolemy II of Egypt, without success. The internal political dynamics of Carthage and the challenges of maintaining control over its African and Sicilian territories further complicated their war efforts.

Notable commanders such as Hamilcar Barca for Carthage and Gaius Lutatius Catulus for Rome played significant roles in various stages of the war. Hamilcar's guerilla tactics in Sicily were notable for their effectiveness in a situation where Carthage could not afford a large standing army.[68]

The war concluded with the decisive Battle of the Aegates in 241 BCE, where the Roman fleet achieved a significant victory over the Carthaginians. The subsequent Treaty of Lutatius was a turning point in the Mediterranean power balance. Carthage evacuated Sicily, handed over prisoners, and agreed to pay a substantial indemnity, marking the end of its dominance in the region. Sicily became Rome's first overseas province, signaling the rise of Rome as a major power and setting the stage for further expansion and future conflicts.

Second Punic War (218-201 BCE)

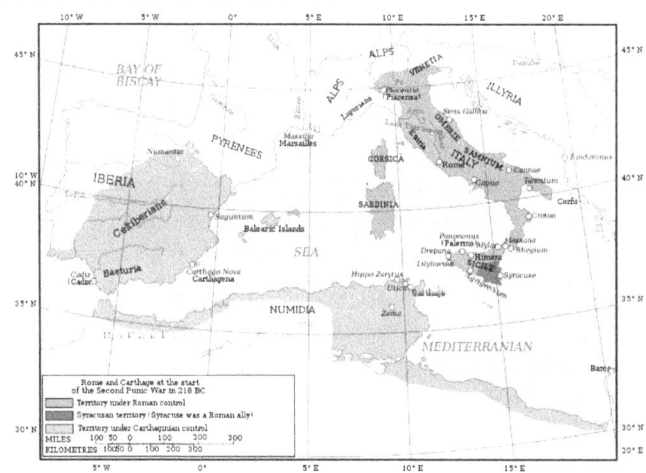

The western Mediterranean in 218 BCE.
Grandiosederivative work: Augusta 89, CC BY-SA 3.0 <https://creativecommons.org/licenses/by-sa/3.0>, via Wikimedia Commons; https://commons.wikimedia.org/wiki/File:Map_of_Rome_and_Carthage_at_the_start_of_the_Second_Punic_War_2.svg

---

[68] Cartwright, M. (2016, May 26). First Punic War. Retrieved from Worldhistory.org: https://www.worldhistory.org/First_Punic_War/.

A legend describes how Hamilcar Barca made his sons swear vengeance on Rome for the humiliating defeat of Carthage in the First Punic War. Whether or not the father demanded this of his sons, one of them, Hannibal, came close to making his father's wish come true in the Second Punic War.

After the First Punic War, Rome and Carthage rapidly expanded their influence, particularly in the western Mediterranean. Because of trade routes, cities, and mineral sources, this region became the new arena of conflict between the two superpowers. The war's outcome would decide the dominant power in the Mediterranean.

The Initial Spark

The war was the culmination of tensions and strategic ambitions between Rome and Carthage. Carthage, which had been defeated and economically burdened by the First Punic War, sought to rebuild its power. Its focus shifted to Spain, a region abundant in resources, which would be crucial for paying off the heavy indemnity to Rome and restoring Carthaginian wealth.

The Barcid family, particularly Hannibal, played a pivotal role in this expansion. Hannibal's personal motivations, fueled by a desire for revenge against Rome, steered Carthage toward a path of confrontation. Hannibal saw conflict with Rome not just as a political strategy but as a personal and nationalistic crusade.

Rome was expanding its influence in the Mediterranean, especially in Spain. Roman interests in Spain were twofold: it wanted the region's rich metal resources, and it wanted to counter Carthaginian expansion. Rome's decision to confront Carthage was significantly influenced by its fear of a potential alliance between Carthage and the Celts in northern Italy. Such an alliance posed a direct threat to Roman security and interests. The Roman Senate saw the growing Carthaginian influence in Spain and the possible alliance with the Celts as a looming threat that needed to be addressed.[69]

The immediate cause of the Second Punic War was Hannibal's siege and capture of Saguntum, a city-state in eastern Spain allied with Rome. Saguntum's strategic and economic importance to Rome's plans in Spain

---

[69] DailyHistory.org. (2024, January 22). What Were the Causes of the Second Punic War? Retrieved from Dailyhistory.org:
https://www.dailyhistory.org/What_were_the_causes_of_the_Second_Punic_War.

made its fall intolerable to the Roman Senate. The Romans demanded Carthage hand over Hannibal for his transgression. Carthage refused, leading to an official declaration of war.[70]

A Military Genius

Hannibal was a general whose name is synonymous with military brilliance. His strategy was expansive and ambitious. He sought to form a global coalition against Rome by rallying forces that feared Rome's rising dominance. By invading Italy, Hannibal aimed to break the aura of Roman invincibility and attract allies, including Greek city-states and Italian rivals of Rome. However, this plan hinged on a critical factor: gaining and maintaining control of Italy, which proved to be Hannibal's greatest challenge.

Hannibal boldly decided not to invade Italy by taking a coastal route along the Mediterranean. Instead, he marched his army across the Alps. His successful trek through the Alpine passes took the Romans by surprise. The Carthaginian commander scored significant victories over larger armies at Ticino, Treba, and Lake Trasimene.

Hannibal's tactical brilliance was undisputed, as exemplified in the Battle of Cannae. Here, he orchestrated one of history's most remarkable military victories, decimating a vast Roman army and inflicting around fifty thousand Roman casualties. Despite this, he decided not to march directly on Rome after Cannae. This decision has been debated among historians for centuries. This choice, seen as a significant misstep, allowed Rome to regroup and ultimately turn the tide of the war.[71]

Despite his early victories, Hannibal faced insurmountable challenges in Italy. His army, though victorious on the battlefield, lacked the manpower and resources to maintain control over the territories. The inability to capture key port cities like Neapolis (Naples) and Tarentum (Taranto) severely hampered his efforts. Moreover, Rome's naval supremacy meant Hannibal could not receive adequate reinforcements or supplies, gradually diminishing his hold over Italian territories.

---

[70] Jones, M. (2024, January 3). The Second Punic War (218-201 BC): Hannibal Marches Against Rome. Retrieved from Historyooperative.org: https://historycooperative.org/second-punic-war-hannibals-war-in-italy/.

[71] Cartwright, M. (2016, May 29). Second Punic War. Retrieved from Worldhistory.org: https://www.worldhistory.org/Second_Punic_War/.

The Romans Adapt

The Romans realized after Cannae that a set battle with Hannibal was a bad idea and that new solutions needed to be tried. Under the leadership of Fabius Maximus, Rome adopted the Fabian strategy, avoiding direct engagement with Hannibal and instead focusing on cutting off his supply lines and isolating him within Italy. This approach of delay and attrition sought to capitalize on Rome's superior resources and manpower. By engaging Hannibal's allies and attacking where he was not present, Rome slowly started to regain the ground it lost.[72]

As the war progressed, its scope widened beyond Italy. Under leaders like Publius Cornelius Scipio (later known as Scipio Africanus), Rome's strategic offensives in Spain significantly weakened Carthage's position. Scipio's military reforms and his adoption of Hannibal's tactics facilitated Roman dominance in Spain. This expansion of the war and the subsequent loss of Spanish territories were detrimental to Carthage's war efforts. Scipio's advance on Carthage caused the Carthaginians to recall Hannibal to defend the homeland.

The Second Punic War culminated with Roman victories in Africa, notably the Battle of Zama, where Scipio defeated Hannibal, earning him the name Africanus. This marked not only the end of the war but also the decline of Carthaginian power and the rise of Rome as the preeminent power in the Mediterranean. Carthage was a beaten state, reduced to a shadow of what it once was.

Third Punic War (149-146 BCE)

The Third Punic War was the final episode of Rome's and Carthage's prolonged struggle. After Carthage's defeat in the previous wars, it found itself heavily restricted. The peace treaty imposed by Rome after the Second Punic War limited Carthage's military capabilities and imposed a heavy indemnity. Despite these limitations, Carthage began to recover economically, which alarmed many in Rome, who still viewed it as a potential threat.

A key figure in the prelude to the Third Punic War was Cato the Elder, a Roman senator known for ending his speeches in the Roman Senate with the warning, "Carthago delenda est!" ("Carthage must be destroyed!"). His concern was not merely the rantings of an old man.

---

[73] Cartwright, M. (2016, May 29). Second Punic War. Retrieved from Worldhistory.org: https://www.worldhistory.org/Second_Punic_War/.

Carthage's recovery threatened Roman commercial interests, particularly those of senators with investments in North Africa. There was also a deep-seated belief in Roman superiority and the perception of Carthage as a civilization that had to be subdued.

Cato's persistence gradually convinced his peers that eliminating Carthage was in Rome's best interests.

The Start of Hostilities

The immediate cause of the Third Punic War can be traced to a conflict between Carthage and the neighboring state of Numidia, a Roman ally. Carthage's decision to defend itself against Numidian incursions violated the treaty with Rome, which forbade Carthage from waging war without Roman consent. This provided Rome with the pretext to declare war.

Anticipating an easy victory, the Romans were met with staunch resistance from the Carthaginians. The prolonged siege of Carthage, led by Roman commander Scipio Aemilianus, eventually cut off Carthage's access to supplies and reinforcements. The Romans constructed a blockade, effectively sealing the city's fate.

As the siege tightened, the situation within Carthage became desperate. In 146 BCE, the Romans launched a final assault. They systematically broke through the city's defenses, and after intense street fighting, they captured and destroyed Carthage. The city was razed, its population enslaved, and a curse was said to be placed on anyone who tried to resettle the area. Carthage's fall marked the end of the Punic Wars and solidified Roman dominance in the western Mediterranean.[73]

---

[73] Cartwright, M. (2016, May 31). Third Punic War. Retrieved from Worldhistory.org: https://www.worldhistory.org/Third_Punic_War/.

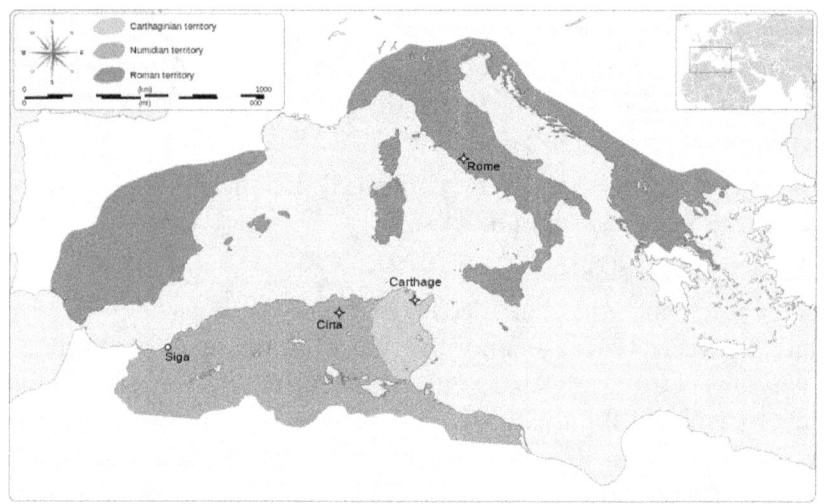

The western Mediterranean in 150 BCE.
Goran tek-en, CC BY-SA 4.0 <https://creativecommons.org/licenses/by-sa/4.0>, via Wikimedia Commons;
https://commons.wikimedia.org/wiki/File:Western_Mediterranean_territory,_150_BC.svg

Carthage would rise again, this time as a Roman provincial city. However, the Punic culture, though maligned by Roman writers, showed remarkable resilience, continuing to influence the region long after the fall of Carthage. This trading empire had remarkable success for centuries and displayed a unique ability to regroup and flourish after a major defeat.

In Summary

The Third Punic War, with its dramatic siege and the final destruction of Carthage, stands as a testament to the ancient world's brutality and the lengths to which states went to eliminate their rivals. The war was not just a military conflict but also a culmination of economic, political, and ideological rivalries that had simmered for over a century. Cato the Elder's relentless advocacy for the war underscores the depth of Roman animosity toward Carthage.

The conflict's legacy is complex, marking the zenith of Roman power in the Mediterranean and a tragic end to a once-great civilization. This war serves as a crucial point of study for understanding the dynamics of power, rivalry, and imperialism in the ancient world.

Chapter 9: Empire of Ghana

West Africa had the Empire of Mali and the Songhai Empire, but these were developed after 1000 CE. There was one, however, that predated the millennium, and that was the Empire of Ghana. It is often referred to as Wagadou. It flourished from the 6th to the 13th century CE and occupied what is now southeastern Mauritania and western Mali; it was not part of what is modern Ghana.

The Empire of Ghana's history is rich and complex, characterized by its strategic position as a hub on trans-Saharan trade routes. Its origins, deeply rooted in the early medieval period, remain somewhat enigmatic with various historical interpretations.

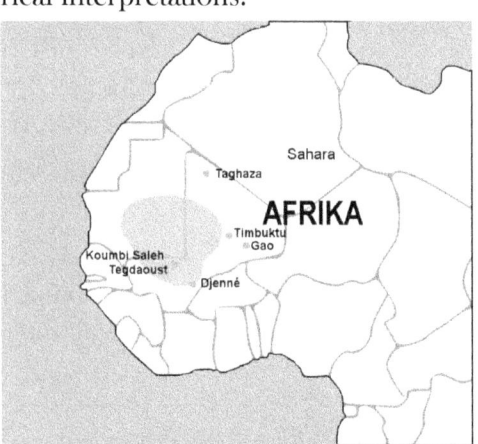

The Ghana Empire at its greatest extent.
Luxo, CC BY-SA 3.0 <http://creativecommons.org/licenses/by-sa/3.0/>, via Wikimedia Commons; https://commons.wikimedia.org/wiki/File:Ghana_empire_map.png

Monarchy and Aristocracy

The monarchy of the Empire of Ghana is shrouded in mystery, with its origins debated among historians. The first identifiable mention of the imperial dynasty was made in 830 by Muhammad ibn Mūsā al-Khwārizmī, with further details provided in the 11th century by the Córdoban scholar al-Bakri.

Historical accounts, such as those by the 11th-century writer al-Idrisi and the 13th-century writer ibn Said, suggest the rulers of Ghana traced their descent from notable figures, including the clan of the Prophet Muhammad. The king, often referred to as "Ghana," a title meaning "Warrior King," was not just a political leader. He also held a religious and cultural role. There were rules about how to behave in his presence, and these had to be obeyed. The guidelines for behavior suggest a high level of ritual surrounding the monarchy. The king had considerable authority over a precious commodity, as he had exclusive rights to own gold nuggets. The merchants were restricted to gold dust. This policy ensured the king could regulate the gold market and maintain its value.

The kings of Ghana relied heavily on advisors from the aristocracy. The ruling class maintained a luxurious and ceremonious court life. The king was adorned with gold and sat before the people in a high cap decorated with gold, surrounded by pages holding shields and swords decorated with gold and flanked by the sons of vassal kings in splendid garments.[74]

The Economy of the Ghana Empire

The Empire of Ghana traded extensively with its neighbors and distant markets. The empire's capital, Koumbi Saleh, was a commercial hub with a business district inhabited by Berber and Arab merchants.[75]

There were several prominent trade goods the empire had ready for market.

- **Gold**

    The principal product traded in the Ghana Empire was gold. Southern regions of the empire were abundant in gold mines,

---

[74] Cartwright, M. (2019, March 5). Ghana Empire. Retrieved from World History Encyclopedia: https://www.worldhistory.org/Ghana_Empire/.

[75] New World Encyclopedia. (2024, January 27). Ghana Empire. Retrieved from New World Encyclopedia: https://www.newworldencyclopedia.org/entry/Ghana_Empire.

making gold an essential component of Ghana's wealth. As mentioned, the kings of Ghana maintained strict control over gold production and trade.

- **Salt**

Salt, sourced mainly from the Sahara, was equally vital to the empire's economy. Salt was not only a precious commodity due to its dietary necessity but also because it was indispensable in preserving food in Africa's hot climate.

- **Slaves**

The Empire of Ghana participated in the slave trade, exchanging slaves for goods with Arab and Berber traders. This aspect of commercial trade was integral to the socioeconomic structures of the region at the time.

The empire traded in various other goods, such as hides, ivory, ostrich feathers, and horses. In exchange, they imported items like textiles, beads, copper, and manufactured goods from the Mediterranean.[76]

Trans-Saharan Trade

The Ghana Empire's economy was predominantly anchored in the lucrative trans-Saharan trade routes. This trade network, enhanced by the introduction of camels to the Sahara Desert in the 3rd century CE, transformed earlier sporadic trade routes into a more structured network running from Morocco to the Niger River. By the 7th century CE, the camel had revolutionized trade across the Sahara, facilitating the transportation of goods across vast desert expanses.

The kings of Ghana played a pivotal role in controlling the trade routes that crisscrossed the empire. They imposed taxes on goods entering and leaving the empire, forming a significant revenue stream that contributed to the kingdom's prosperity. The empire's strategic location, sandwiched between gold fields to the south and salt mines to the north, allowed it to act as a trading hub where these valuable commodities were exchanged.

The taxation system in the Ghana Empire was unique and innovative for its time. Instead of money, the king imposed a percentage fee on

---

[76] Cartwright, M. (2019, March 5). Ghana Empire. Retrieved from World History Encyclopedia: https://www.worldhistory.org/Ghana_Empire/.

importers and exporters that was paid by their trade goods. Consequently, a given trade commodity was often taxed twice, once upon entry and again upon exit from the empire.[77] In addition, Ghana received income from surrounding tributary states. The tax and tribute system added to the coffers of the treasury and helped the empire control trade in commodities such as salt and gold.

Ghana's location in the upper valley of the Niger River permitted it to have access to all the major trade routes. The trade in gold, salt, and slaves passed through the empire along two very important routes:

- The trade route that connected the capital of the Ghana Empire, Koumbi Saleh, to cities like Aoudaghost (Awdaghust) and Sijilmasa.
- The route to the iron ore and gold-producing areas in the south, particularly the Bambuk and Bure regions, which stretched into the empire's heartland.[78]

The wealth generated from trade led to significant urban development within the empire. Koumbi Saleh emerged as a major trade center, boasting numerous mosques and a vibrant mix of different cultures. This economic prosperity further facilitated the development of other urban centers across the empire.[79]

Islam in the Ghana Empire

There was a very significant cultural import that came from the trans-Saharan trade routes: Islam. Muslim merchants and traders introduced the religion to the Empire of Ghana in the 8th century CE, although it did not become a prominent religion until later. Commerce permitted Islam to develop and thrive, even though the monarchy retained its ties with the older religious customs.

---

[77] Cartwright, M. (2019, March 5). Ghana Empire. Retrieved from World History Encyclopedia: https://www.worldhistory.org/Ghana_Empire/.

[78] Cartwright, M. (2019, May 13). The Gold Trade of Ancient & Medieval West Africa. Retrieved from Worldhistory.org: https://www.worldhistory.org/article/1383/the-gold-trade-of-ancient-medieval-west-africa/.

[79] LibreTexts. (2024, January 27). 12.6 The Ghana Empire. Retrieved from LibreTexts.org: https://human.libretexts.org/Courses/Lumen_Learning/Book%3A_Early_World_Civilizations_(Lumen)/Ch._11_African_Civilizations/12.6%3A_The_Ghana_Empire#:~:text=Ghana%E2%80%99s%20economic%20development%20and%20eventual%20wealth%20was%20linked,expansion%20to%20.

The king relied on advisors and officials to manage the economy and monitor trade activities. This included Muslim merchants acting as interpreters and officials, signifying the empire's economic complexity and its integration into the broader Islamic world.

Numerous scribes and ministers in the bureaucracy were Muslim, allowing them to have an essential role in the daily functioning of the empire. Islam brought with it the Arabic language, Islamic teachings, and scientific knowledge. The cities benefited culturally from the influx of learning that came with the Muslim merchants.[80]

The economic prosperity of the Empire of Ghana was also enhanced by its association with Muslim merchants. Muslim traders, particularly the Sanhaja Berbers, were central to the trans-Saharan trade network, facilitating the exchange of gold from West Africa for salt and other goods from North Africa.[81]

The kings of Ghana, while predominantly adhering to traditional religious beliefs, demonstrated a remarkable tolerance toward Islam, allowing for a symbiotic relationship between the two cultures. This approach of tolerance underlines the pragmatic nature of Ghana's rulers, who sought to harness the administrative and intellectual expertise of Muslims to enhance governance. Their understanding and respect for another religion demonstrate how cultures and religions can interact to their mutual benefit and improve the stability and prosperity of a nation.

The Fall of the Empire

In spite of great economic prosperity and a tolerant society, the Empire of Ghana eventually collapsed. It was not because of one catastrophe; a series of disasters hit Ghana. The ruling class was unable to come up with solutions that could have saved this civilization.

---

[80] Encyclopedia.com. (2024, January 27). Empire of Ghana. Retrieved from Encyclopedia.com: https://www.encyclopedia.com/history/encyclopedias-almanacs-transcripts-and-maps/empire-ghana.

[81] Lane, M. (2024, January 21). How Did Muslims and Non-Muslims Interact in Ghana. Retrieved from Ncesc.com: https://www.ncesc.com/geographic-faq/how-did-muslims-and-non-muslims-interact-in-ghana/.

These were the principal reasons for Ghana's demise:
- External Invasions and Wars

  Regrettably, Islam brought challenges along with benefits. In 1076, the Almoravids, a Berber Muslim dynasty from the Sahara, invaded and defeated Ghana's army. This defeat weakened the empire's military strength and accelerated the spread of Islam, further exacerbating internal religious tensions. Following this, the Susu Kingdom attacked in 1203, eroding Ghana's military and economic authority in the region. These military defeats were crucial in diminishing the empire's ability to control its territories and maintain its economic dominance.

  The final collapse of the Empire of Ghana can be attributed to the rise of the Mali Empire, which gradually became more prominent in the region. In 1240, the Mali emperor, Sundiata, conquered what was left of the Ghana Empire and incorporated it into the Mali Empire. This marked the end of Ghana as a political entity and the rise of a new regional power.

- Economic Changes

  Ghana relied heavily on trade and the taxes derived from trans-Saharan trade. New routes were developed that bypassed Ghana. Additionally, the natural environment became a challenge.

- Climate Changes

  Significant climatic changes happened in the 12th century, and the region became gradually drier. This prolonged drought affected agricultural production, undermining the empire's ability to sustain itself and its population. The agricultural decline would have a ripple effect on the economy, further destabilizing the already weakened empire.[82]

- Dissension within the Borders

  Other internal factors were political instability and social unrest. The empire faced internal conflicts and growing dissatisfaction with the central government. There was a desire among member states for independence or alignment with other rising

---

[82] Cartwright, M. (2019, March 5). Ghana Empire. Retrieved from World History Encyclopedia: https://www.worldhistory.org/Ghana_Empire/.

powers, like Mali.

Additionally, the empire grappled with the inherent conflict between traditional beliefs and the growing influence of Islam. These religious and cultural tensions weakened the social and political cohesion of the empire.

The final blows Sundiata inflicted were on an imperial state whose structure was shaky and whose foundations had been severely weakened. The empire was no longer able to resist. What was left of the empire was incorporated into the Mali Empire. Ghana ceased to be a political entity, and the new authority in the region grew increasingly more powerful.[83]

<u>In Summary</u>

The Empire of Ghana is a remarkable saga in the history of West Africa, showing how control over strategic trade routes and resources with high consumer demand can sustain a powerful state. The empire's sophisticated economy and tax system facilitated its rise to power and prosperity while connecting West Africa to the rest of the medieval world. The decline of Ghana marked the end of an amazing empire located in the desert sands.

This discussion of Ghana is intended to remind the reader that the northern coast of Africa and the Nile Valley were not the only places where civilization flourished on the continent.

---

[83] Soto, N. (2024, January 16). Who Destroyed the Ghana Empire. Retrieved from Ncesc.com: https://www.ncesc.com/geographic-faq/who-destroyed-the-ghana-empire/.

Chapter 10: Slavery in Ancient Africa

An honest history of Africa must mention slavery. Slavery has plagued the continent for centuries and spawned the trans-Saharan slave trade and the later transatlantic slave trade.

The history of slavery in ancient Africa is complex and was shaped by the cultures and practices of various African civilizations. Forms of slavery included debt bondage, military slavery, the enslavement of war captives, and domestic servitude.

- Debt Slavery

  People who were unable to repay debts would be forced into servitude. Unlike other forms of slavery, debt slavery was often seen as a temporary and more humane solution for debtors. Debt slavery was common in West Africa among the Yoruba, Ga, Ewe, and Edo cultures. It was also common in ancient Egypt.

- Military Slavery

  Military slavery involved the recruitment and utilization of enslaved individuals as soldiers. This practice was prominent in certain African states, where enslaved soldiers formed an integral part of the military force. These individuals could rise to significant ranks and often held considerable power. In ancient Egypt, slaves were used as soldiers and guards. A later example would be the Mamluks, who eventually overthrew the

Ayyubid dynasty and became the rulers of Egypt.[84]

- Enslavement of War Captives

The capture and enslavement of prisoners of war was a widespread practice in ancient Africa. This form of slavery was the outcome of military conflicts and raids, and both Carthage and Egypt used prisoners of war as forced laborers. The slave trade in West Africa encouraged the use of raids and wars to gather a supply of prisoners to be sold.

Slavery in Ancient Egypt

A major source of enslaved people in ancient Egypt were prisoners captured from conquered lands during military expeditions. The victors often took captives back to Egypt to serve as slaves. Criminals and convicted individuals were sometimes sentenced to slavery as a form of punishment, and individuals could become slaves due to debts they could not repay.

Humans were a commercial commodity, and Egyptians would trade luxury items for captured humans. Slaves could also be acquired as gifts or tribute.

Slavery was hereditary in ancient Egypt, meaning children born to enslaved individuals would also be considered slaves.

A Slave's Life in Egypt

Slaves in ancient Egypt performed various tasks based on their assigned roles. They worked in agriculture, tending to fields and livestock, and in construction. Although slaves likely were involved in some building projects, modern-day scholars do not believe they worked on monumental structures like the pyramids due to the evidence of organized living quarters, a regular diet, and access to medical care and other necessities.

The living conditions of slaves varied depending on their roles and the social status of their owners. Of course, the working conditions could be harsh, but slaves did have certain legal rights and could own property.[85] Carthage allowed slaves to run businesses for their masters.

---

[84] Britannica, E. o. (2023, November 30). Mamluk. Retrieved from Britannica.com: https://www.britannica.com/topic/Mamluk.

[85] Historyrise.com. (2023, December 24). Facts About Ancient Egypt Slaves: Historical Insights! Retrieved from Historyrise.com: https://historyrise.com/facts-about-ancient-egypt-slaves/.

Slavery in the Kingdoms of Kerma and Punt

A significant challenge in analyzing slavery in the cultures of Kerma and Punt is the lack of records. We have to wait for archaeology to uncover information about the practice of enforced labor in these civilizations. We know that Egypt had a significant influence on the region. It is possible that slavery was conducted with customs that emulated those of the land of the pharaohs.

Slavery in Carthage

In Carthage, slavery had profound socioeconomic impacts. It facilitated large-scale agricultural and architectural projects, bolstered military campaigns, and was a cornerstone in trade relations.

Slavery was central to the Carthaginian economy, something that mirrored the practices of many other ancient civilizations. The enslaved were primarily conquered peoples and those bought from slave markets. The integration of enslaved people into Carthaginian society reflected the city's many military conquests and active participation in regional trade, including the slave trade.[86]

Slaves were employed in numerous professions. These might be domestic services or skilled labor in agriculture, craftsmanship, and maritime trade. Slaves were even used in the Carthaginian navy during the Punic Wars. The larger workshops in Carthage, which produced a range of goods from pottery to metalwork, employed both citizens and slaves. The presence of slaves in these workshops highlights their integral role in the Carthaginian economy.

The economic structure of Carthage was heavily dependent on slave labor. Slaves played a crucial role in the city's manufacturing sector, including textiles, pottery, and metalwork production. In agriculture, slave labor was instrumental in maintaining Carthage's agricultural output. Slaves were an essential part of the workforce. Slave labor allowed Carthaginian landowners to maximize agricultural production, contributing to the city's overall economic prosperity.

---

[86] LibreTexts. (2024, January 22). 4.2 Ancient Carthage. Retrieved from Libretexts.org: https://human.libretexts.org/Courses/Lumen_Learning/Book%3A_Early_World_Civilizations_(Lumen)/Ch._03_Early_Civilizations_of_Africa_and_the_Andes/04.2%3A_Ancient_Carthage.

The Status of Enslaved People

The relationship between slaves and their owners in Carthage was not uniformly oppressive. In some situations, slaves were allowed to run businesses for their masters with a degree of autonomy. This implies that while slaves were not free, they could engage in economic activities independently. Some slaves were even able to accumulate personal wealth, albeit likely under the oversight of their masters.

Despite slave revolts in the 4th century BCE, there is little evidence of widespread or continual unrest among the slave population in Carthage. This lack of significant unrest could be attributed to various factors, including the possibility of earning freedom or better treatment than other contemporary slave-owning societies.[87]

Slavery in Aksum

Slavery was an integral part of social and economic life in Aksum, as it was in many ancient societies. Slaves were primarily drawn from the Nilotic groups of Ethiopia's southern hinterland and the Oromo people. War captives constituted another considerable source of slaves. These individuals were assimilated into various societal roles, serving as concubines, bodyguards, servants, and treasurers. Despite the scarcity of detailed records, it's clear that slavery was deeply embedded in Aksum's social fabric.

The port of Adulis was a renowned hub for the slave trade, connecting the empire to a global market for slaves for many centuries. The involvement in such trade networks suggests external trade influenced the supply and demand of enslaved people as much as internal needs.

Aksum had a feudal society, with land ownership and agriculture playing pivotal roles. Slaves were instrumental in this system, working the land alongside free peasants. The empire's reliance on agriculture for its economy, with principal crops being grains like wheat and barley, necessitated a labor force that included slaves.

Aksum converted to Christianity in the 4th century CE. It is plausible that Christian morals and ethics might have influenced the treatment of

---

[87] Cartwright, M. (2016, June 16). Carthaginian Society. Retrieved from Worldhistory.org: https://www.worldhistory.org/article/908/carthaginian-society/.

slaves, but concrete evidence is limited.[88]

The Ancient African View of Slavery

We know about the slave trade in Africa from historical records, but many accounts date from after 1000 CE. Later West African empires, like the Ghana Empire, were deeply involved in the trans-Saharan slave trade, and later kingdoms were active participants in the transatlantic slave trade. However, the roots of slavery go back centuries before the Empire of Mali or the arrival of the Europeans. The early days are worth investigating.

The uniqueness of African slavery lay in its integration with kinship and societal structures. Unlike chattel slavery in the Americas, African slavery often involved complex relationships with certain rights and freedoms for the enslaved. The degree of leniency and the nature of treatment varied, often influenced by the slave's origin and whether they were born into slavery or acquired through purchase or war.

African societies utilized slavery as a means to enhance personal influence and societal connections, particularly in regions where land ownership was not a concept. This practice entrenched slaves within the master's lineage, occasionally allowing their offspring to ascend to significant societal positions, even to the chieftaincy. However, this integration did not erase the inherent stigma, and clear distinctions between enslaved people and the master's blood relatives were often maintained.

Moral opposition to slavery was nuanced. The indigenous forms of slavery, which were often less severe than the chattel slavery later established in the Americas, did not always elicit the same level of moral outrage. In some African societies, slavery was justified through cultural and religious beliefs. The enslavement of war captives, for instance, was often seen as a natural consequence of conflict. Moreover, the integration of slaves into the master's lineage in some cultures provided a form of social mobility, albeit limited, blurring the lines between pure exploitation and social integration.

While there was no widespread moral opposition to slavery akin to the later abolitionist movements, African societies exhibited a range of attitudes toward slavery, from acceptance as a social norm to forms of

---

[88] New World Encyclopedia. (2024, January 25). Aksumite Empire. Retrieved from NewWorldEncuclopedia.org: https://www.newworldencyclopedia.org/entry/Aksumite_Empire.

resistance and adaptation in response to internal and external changes.

<u>In Summary</u>

Slavery in ancient Africa was not a monolith but rather a spectrum of practices influenced by cultural, economic, and environmental factors. Each civilization, from Egypt, Carthage, and Punt to Kerma and Kush, had its own distinct forms of slavery, shaped by its unique circumstances and interactions with neighboring regions. Understanding these nuances provides valuable insights into the complex account of ancient African history.

Conclusion

"Take up the White Man's burden—
Send forth the best ye breed—
Go bind your sons to exile
To serve your captives' need;
To wait in heavy harness
On fluttered folk and wild—
Your new-caught, sullen peoples,
Half devil and half child.
Take up the White Man's burden—
In patience to abide,
To veil the threat of terror
And check the show of pride;
By open speech and simple,
An hundred times made plain.
To seek another's profit,
And work another's gain.
Take up the White Man's burden—
And reap his old reward:
The blame of those ye better,
The hate of those ye guard—

The cry of hosts ye humour
(Ah, slowly!) toward the light:—
'Why brought ye us from bondage,
 Our loved Egyptian night?'"
The White Man's Burden by Rudyard Kipling[89]

Europe carved up Africa in the late 19th century, justifying a naked land grab by insisting that the continent needed the gift of civilization that only it, Europe, could bestow. Africa was caught in a moment of weakness, and its nations could not adequately combat the technological and financial might of Great Britain, France, Germany, Italy, and Belgium. Africans would become part of empires whose people looked different and spoke alien languages.

The arrogance and condescension of these new masters was palpable. Europeans initially ignored the ruins of ancient imperial dynasties and assumed the native populations were primitive tribes or religious fanatics. Writers speculated that the Portuguese or Chinese built Great Zimbabwe, a city in Zimbabwe that is believed to have served as a capital during the Iron Age. Such notions stem from biased observations that the local population was incapable of academic discourse or building massive stone structures. It would take years of archaeological excavations before those ideas were dismissed as false.[90]

Ancient Africa was more than jungle and half-naked savages. European hegemony could not hide the continent's contributions to humanity over the centuries.

Metallurgy and Chemistry

The Age of Metals underscores Africa's invaluable contributions to metallurgy and chemistry. The skillful manipulation of metals by the Egyptians and the later Edo people, exemplified in artifacts like the Benin Bronzes, showcases advanced techniques in metalworking. Moreover, the ancient practice of alchemy in Egypt, which significantly influenced the Greeks and Asians, is a precursor to modern chemistry.

---

[89] Kipling, Rudyard (1899). The White Man's Burden. https://historymatters.gmu.edu/d/5478/.

[90] Koutonin, M. (2016, August 18). Lost Cities: Racism and Ruins—The Plundering of Great Zimbabwe. Retrieved from Theguardian.com:
https://www.theguardian.com/cities/2016/aug/18/great-zimbabwe-medieval-lost-city-racism-ruins-plundering.

This early knowledge of chemistry and metallurgy, vital to human progress, underscores Africa's role in advancing scientific knowledge.

Astronomy

African civilizations made groundbreaking strides in astronomy. The inhabitants of Nabta Playa created one of the world's first astronomical observatories, predating Stonehenge. Their Rock Calendar was a significant innovation for tracking celestial movements and is reportedly older than Stonehenge. Furthermore, the Dogon people of Mali were known for their detailed understanding of astronomical phenomena, notably the Sirius star system. These achievements in astronomy not only highlight Africa's scientific prowess but also its contribution to our knowledge of the cosmos.[91]

Egyptians integrated astronomy into their culture, with the best example being the Great Pyramid of Giza. The pyramid was aligned with celestial bodies. Its air shafts, pointing toward stars like Sirius and the Orion constellation, underscore the significance of these heavenly bodies in Egyptian mythology and religious practices. In addition, the alignments were used to mark the times of the year for planting and harvesting.[92]

Education

The Library of Alexandria comes to attention immediately when thinking about the advancement of knowledge. However, it was not the only African library; Alexandria was just one of many intellectual centers on the continent. The city of Timbuktu, part of the later Mali Empire, became a significant center of Islamic learning. Timbuktu had the University of Sankore, the Sidi Yahya Mosque, and the Djinguereber Mosque. Another academic center of ancient Africa was the Axumite imperial church. These prove the colonial notion of Africa being an illiterate continent false.

Mathematics

The mathematical practices of ancient Africa have contributed significantly to the global understanding of mathematics. An astonishing

---

[91] Afrikaiswoke.com. (2023, September 15). 10 African Contributions to Civilization. Retrieved from Afrikaiswoke.com: https://www.afrikaiswoke.com/african-contributions-to-civilization/.

[92] Shuttleworth, M. (2024, January 28). Egyptian Astronomy. Retrieved from Explorable.com: https://explorable.com/egyptian-astronomy.

example of the use of mathematics in pre-modern Africa is the Lebombo bone. This baboon fibula, discovered in the Lebombo Mountains of southern Africa and carved in prehistoric times, has twenty-nine deliberate notches that possibly represent an ancient lunar phase counter.

The Yoruba tribe of Nigeria developed a numeration system, a base-20 system that integrated subtraction for number expression and was operational up to two hundred. This system demonstrated abstract mathematical reasoning tailored to the needs of the tribe.[93]

We usually think of Mesopotamia and India regarding numbers, but Egypt left a mathematical legacy that significantly advanced the study of mathematics. A non-positional decimal system characterized ancient Egyptian mathematics. Their numerals, represented by distinct hieroglyphs for each power of ten up to one million, were effective for their needs and revealed an early abstraction of quantitative concepts.

The Rhind Mathematical Papyrus provides evidence of the practical nature of Egyptian mathematics. Along with other scrolls, the texts consider problems of land measurement, construction, and resource distribution.

The Egyptians showed an advanced understanding of algebra and used its methods to solve linear equations and arithmetic progressions. Their problem-solving techniques, including the method of false position, show an ability to approach mathematical problems systematically, showcasing advanced mathematical thinking. They had a deep understanding of geometry, calculating areas and volumes and applying these calculations to real-world problems.[94]

Medicine

Medicine in Africa goes beyond shaman chants and plants. Ancient African civilizations were pioneers in the field of medicine. They blended empirical knowledge and traditional practices to promote health and healing.

---

[93] Anplifyafrica.org. (2024, January 28). Africa Made Math: The Original Mathematicians. Retrieved from Anplifyafrica.org: https://www.amplifyafrica.org/africa-made-math-the-original-mathematicians/.

[94] Historyrise.com. (2023, December 25). What Advancements Did Ancient Egypt Make in Math and Science. Retrieved from Historyrise.com: https://historyrise.com/advancements-in-ancient-egyptian-math-science/.

Procedures performed in ancient Africa before they were known in Europe include inoculations, mummification, limb traction, bone settings, brain surgeries, skin grafting, the filling of dental cavities, the installation of false teeth, anesthesia, and tissue cauterization. African cultures also performed surgeries under antiseptic conditions.

Ancient African societies employed many medical procedures that are used today. They utilized plants with salicylic acid for pain, kaolin for diarrhea, and extracts to kill gram-positive bacteria. Some plants had anti-cancer properties, could induce abortion, or were used to treat malaria. Africans discovered compounds like ouabain, capsicum, physostigmine, and reserpine, which had significant medical applications.[95]

Architecture and Engineering

The architectural and engineering feats of ancient African civilizations are a testament to their sophistication. From the towering pyramids and obelisks of Egypt to the grand stone complexes in Zimbabwe and Mozambique, African societies demonstrated advanced construction and urban planning knowledge. The stone structures of Great Zimbabwe are a testament to the ingenuity and skill of its builders. The later Empire of Mali, particularly its renowned city of Timbuktu, boasted impressive architectural structures, including grand palaces, mosques, and universities. These structures were not only marvels of engineering but also centers of cultural and intellectual exchange.[96]

Further Study

What we now know about Africa prior to the arrival of the Europeans refutes the colonial ideas of an uneducated continent. Nevertheless, there is still much more to learn about Africa. There are many mysteries waiting to be solved and secrets waiting to be uncovered. The investigation should be multi-faceted and include archaeological excavations, genetic research, and linguistic studies. This approach not

---

[95] Blatch, S. (2013, February 1). Great Achievements in Science and Technology in Ancient Africa. Retrieved from Asbmb.org: https://www.asbmb.org/asbmb-today/science/020113/great-achievements-in-stem-in-ancient-africa

[96] Exponent, E. (2023, November 14). Ancient Africa's Contributions to Modern Science and Built Environment. Retrieved from The African Exponent: https://www.africanexponent.com/ancient-africas-contributions-to-modern-science-and-built-environment/.

only aids in constructing a more comprehensive historical narrative but also ensures that the research is inclusive and respects the region's cultural heritage.

Archaeological endeavors in regions like Great Zimbabwe and the kingdoms of the Sahel have the potential to uncover artifacts and structures that can provide insights into these societies' daily lives, social structures, and technological advancements. Great Zimbabwe's buildings, with their intricate designs and construction techniques, could offer clues about the engineering skills of central Africa. Similarly, excavations in the Nile Valley and other historical sites could reveal new aspects of trade networks and cultural exchanges within Africa. Recent studies have identified traces of ancient African empires in the DNA of contemporary African populations. Further investigations will help explain the migration and interactions of people across the continent.

Linguistic analysis can reveal aspects of social organization, religious beliefs, culture, and the intellectual lives of civilizations that no longer exist. Breaking the language code of Great Zimbabwe may lead to some startling discoveries that could destroy contemporary ideas. That was the case with the Maya civilization. Initially, scholars thought the Maya were a peaceful society of stargazers. Their ability to finally interpret the glyphs found in Maya temples and monuments showed the people engaged in almost continuous warfare. What little we know about Great Zimbabwe might be wrong, and we must be ready to accept that possibility.

The religious beliefs, artistic expressions, and cultural practices of ancient African societies still need to be fully understood. Excavating worship sites, burial grounds, and artistic creations could offer a window into these societies' spiritual and cultural life. Looking further into the trans-Saharan trade, Indian Ocean trade networks, and intra-African trade dynamics could give us better insights into the continent's role in the global economy. Analyzing historic climate change has allowed us to better understand decisions made by the Maya and Khmer civilizations. Researching how ancient African empires adapted and responded to environmental fluctuations can offer insights into farming, climate change responses, and the impact of human activities on the environment.

The history of ancient African empires is a saga of human achievement and interaction. Further research of these societies is not just an academic pursuit but also a quest for a more inclusive and comprehensive understanding of human history. By exploring unanswered questions and uncharted territories, we stand to gain a deeper appreciation of the continent's rich heritage and its significant contributions to the story of humanity.

If you enjoyed this book, a review on Amazon would be greatly appreciated because it would mean a lot to hear from you.

To leave a review:
1. Open your camera app.
2. Point your mobile device at the QR code.
3. The review page will appear in your web browser.

Thanks for your support!

Here's another book by Enthralling History that you might like

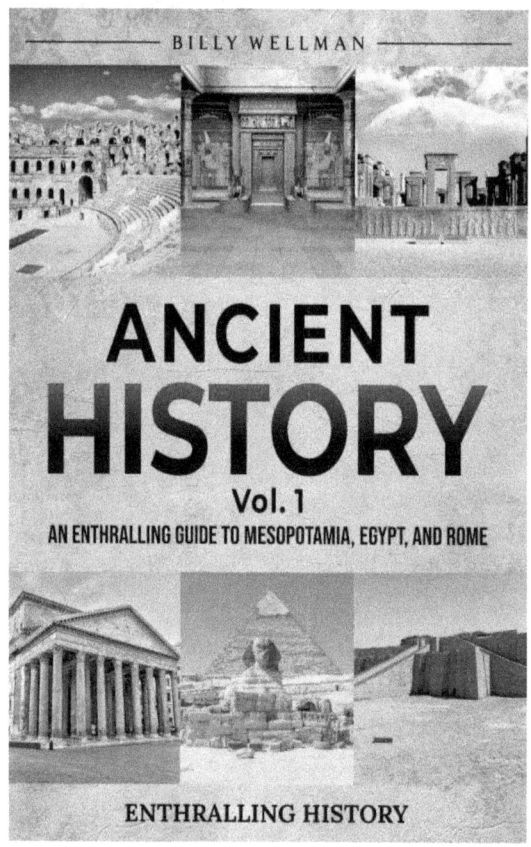

Free limited time bonus

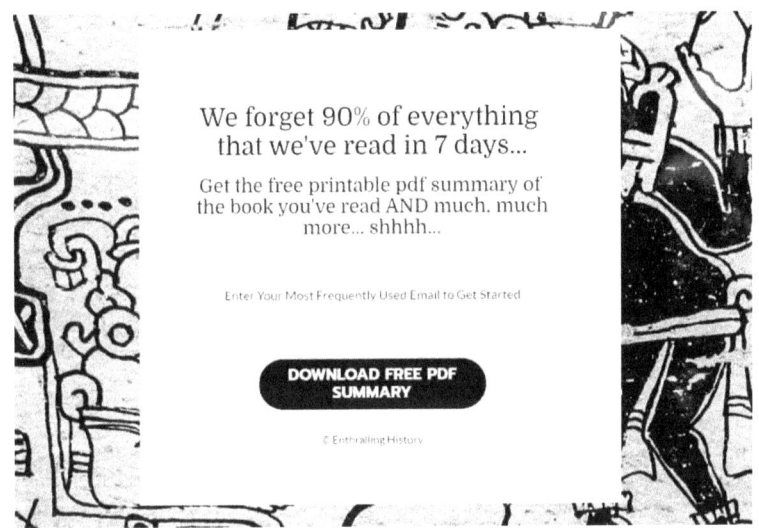

Stop for a moment. We have a free bonus set up for you. The problem is this: we forget 90% of everything that we read after 7 days. Crazy fact, right? Here's the solution: we've created a printable, 1-page pdf summary for this book that you're reading now. All you have to do to get your free pdf summary is to go to the following website: https://livetolearn.lpages.co/enthrallinghistory/

Or, Scan the QR code!

Once you do, it will be intuitive. Enjoy, and thank you!

Bibliography

Academic Accelerator. (2024, January 13). Archaeological Evidence for the Origins and Spread of Iron Production in Africa. Retrieved from Academic-accelerator.com: https://academic-accelerator.com/encyclopedia/iron-metallurgy-in-africa.

Afrikaiswoke.com. (2023, September 15). 10 African Contributions to Civilization. Retrieved from Afrikaiswoke.com: https://www.afrikaiswoke.com/african-contributions-to-civilization/.

Ancient Egypt Magazine. (2023, February 6). Neolithic Settlements of the Western Desert: Proto-villages of Stone Age Egypt. Retrieved from the-past.com: https://the-past.com/feature/neolithic-settlements-of-the-western-desert-proto-villages-of-stone-age-egypt/.

Ancientegptianfacts.com. (2024, January 19). Facts About Ancient Egyptians. Retrieved from Ancientegptianfacts.com: https://ancientegyptianfacts.com/ptolemaic-period-egypt.html.

Anplifyafrica.org. (2024, January 28). Africa Made Math: The Original Mathematicians. Retrieved from Anplifyafrica.org: https://www.amplifyafrica.org/africa-made-math-the-original-mathematicians/.

Bevan, E. (2024, January 19). Chapter IV: The People, the Cities, the Court. Retrieved from Penelope.uchicago.edu: https://penelope.uchicago.edu/Thayer/E/Gazetteer/Places/Africa/Egypt/_Texts/BEVHOP/4B*.html.

Blatch, S. (2013, February 1). Great Achievements in Science and Technology in Ancient Africa. Retrieved from Asbmb.org: https://www.asbmb.org/asbmb-today/science/020113/great-achievements-in-stem-in-ancient-africa.

Brewminate.com. (2019, April 17). The Art and Architecture of Middle Kingdom Egypt c. 2055-1650 BCE. Retrieved from brewminate.com: https://brewminate.com/the-art-and-architecture-of-middle-kingdom-egypt-c-2055-1650-bce/.

Brewminate.com. (2019, April 19). The Art and Architecture of New Kingdom Egypt c. 1570-1069.BCE. Retrieved from brewmintate.com: https://brewminate.com/the-art-and-architecture-of-new-kingdom-egypt-c-1570-1069-bce/.

Britannica, E. o. (2023, November 30). Mamluk. Retrieved from Britannica.com: https://www.britannica.com/topic/Mamluk.

Cartwright, M. (2016, June 16). Carthaginian Society. Retrieved from Worldhistory.org: https://www.worldhistory.org/article/908/carthaginian-society/.

Cartwright, M. (2016, June 17). Carthaginian Trade. Retrieved from Worldhistory.org: https://www.worldhistory.org/article/911/carthaginian-trade/.

Cartwright, M. (2016, May 26). First Punic War. Retrieved from Worldhistory.org: https://www.worldhistory.org/First_Punic_War/.

Cartwright, M. (2016, May 29). Second Punic War. Retrieved from Worldhistory.org: https://www.worldhistory.org/Second_Punic_War/.

Cartwright, M. (2016, May 31). Third Punic War. Retrieved from Worldhistory.org: https://www.worldhistory.org/Third_Punic_War/.

Cartwright, M. (2018, July 24). Lighthouse of Alexandria. Retrieved from Worldhistory.org: https://www.worldhistory.org/Lighthouse_of_Alexandria/.

Cartwright, M. (2019, March 5). Ghana Empire. Retrieved from World History Encyclopedia: https://www.worldhistory.org/Ghana_Empire/.

Cartwright, M. (2019, March 21). Kingdom of Axum. Retrieved from Worldhistory.org: https://www.worldhistory.org/Kingdom_of_Axum/.

Cartwright, M. (2019, May 13). The Gold Trade of Ancient & Medieval West Africa. Retrieved from Worldhistory.org: https://www.worldhistory.org/article/1383/the-gold-trade-of-ancient--medieval-west-africa/.

Cartwright, M. (2916, January 8). Carthaginian Army. Retrieved from Worldhistory.org: https://www.worldhistory.org/Carthaginian_Army/.

Cassar, C. (2023, August 25). Exploring the Egyptian Middle Kingdom—A Historical Overview. Retrieved from Anthropologureview.org: https://anthropologyreview.org/history/ancient-egypt/exploring-the-egyptian-middle-kingdom-a-historical-overview/?expand_article=1.

Cerise Myers, E. C. (2024, January 9). 5.2 Mesolithic Art. Retrieved from Libretexts.org: https://human.libretexts.org/Bookshelves/Art/Introduction_to_Art_History_I_%28Myers%29/05%3A_Art_of_the_Stone_Age/5.02%3A_Mesolithic_Art.

College Sidekick.com. (2024, January 13). The Bronze Age. Retrieved from Collegesidekick.com: https://www.collegesidekick.com/study-guides/boundless-arthistory/the-bronze-age.

DailyHistory.org. (2024, January 22). What Were the Causes of the Second Punic War? Retrieved from Dailyhistory.org: https://www.dailyhistory.org/What_were_the_causes_of_the_Second_Punic_War.

DeMola, P. (2013, March 14). Interrelations of Kerma and Pharaonic Egypt. Retrieved from World History Encyclopedia: https://www.worldhistory.org/article/487/interrelations-of-kerma-and-pharaonic-egypt/.

Dickinson College Commentaries. (2024, January 22). Carthage: Early History. Retrieved from dcc.dickoinson.edu: https://dcc.dickinson.edu/nepos-hannibal/carthage-early-history.

Editors, H. (2013, June 12). Punic Wars. Retrieved from Hisory.com: https://www.history.com/topics/ancient-rome/punic-wars#first-punic-war-264-241-b-c.

EDU, W. H. (2023, May 10). Aristotle's Analysis of the Carthaginian Constitution. Retrieved from Worldhistory.edu: https://worldhistoryedu.com/aristotles-analysis-of-the-carthaginian-constitution/.

Encyclopedia.com. (2024, January 27). Empire of Ghana. Retrieved from Encyclopedia.com: https://www.encyclopedia.com/history/encyclopedias-almanacs-transcripts-and-maps/empire-ghana.

EOTC. (2024, January 13). Beliefs and Teachings of Ethiopian Orthodox Tewahedo Church. Retrieved from keraneyo-medhanealem.com: https://www.keraneyo-medhanealem.com/beliefs-and-origins-7-sacraments-of.

Eries.org. (2024, January 13). Kingdom of Aksum. Retrieved from Eriesd.org: https://www.eriesd.org/cms/lib/PA01001942/Centricity/Domain/1041/6.2%20The%20Kingdom%20of%20Aksum-1.pdf.

Exponent, E. (2023, November 14). Ancient Africa's Contributions to Modern Science and Built Environment. Retrieved from The African Exponent: https://www.africanexponent.com/ancient-africas-contributions-to-modern-science-and-built-environment/.

Fitzgerald, S. (2023, November 21). Mummified Baboons in Egypt Point to a Long Lost Land. Retrieved from Atlas Obscura: https://www.atlasobscura.com/articles/mummified-baboons-punt.

Haughton, B. (2011, February 1). What Happened to the Great Library at Alexandria? Retrieved from Worldhistory.org: https://www.worldhistory.org/article/207/what-happened-to-the-great-library-at-alexandria/.

Hirst, K. (2019, May 12). The Kingdom of Kush: Sub-Saharan African Rulers of the Nile. Retrieved from Thoughtco.com: https://www.thoughtco.com/the-kingdom-of-kush-171464.

Historyskills.com. (2024, January 19). What Was the Middle Kingdom of Ancient Egypt? Retrieved from Historyskills.com: https://www.historyskills.com/classroom/ancient-history/anc-middle-kingdom-reading/.

Historyrise.com. (2023, December 24). Facts About Ancient Egypt Slaves: Historical Insights! Retrieved from Historyrise.com: https://historyrise.com/facts-about-ancient-egypt-slaves/.

Historyrise.com. (2023, December 25). What Advancements Did Ancient Egypt Make in Math and Science. Retrieved from Historyrise.com: https://historyrise.com/advancements-in-ancient-egyptian-math-science/.

Historyskills.com. (2024, January 19). How Egypt Became the Greatest Superpower of the Ancient World. Retrieved from Hisoryskills.com: https://www.historyskills.com/classroom/ancient-history/egypt-ancient-superpower/.

Hunt, P. (2024, January 22). Carthage. Retrieved from Britannica.com: https://www.britannica.com/place/Carthage-ancient-city-Tunisia.

Huysecom, E. (2024, January 9). Arguments for an Early Neolithic in Sub-Saharan Africa. Retrieved from Ounjougou.org: https://www.ounjougou.org/en/projects/mali/archaeology/arguments-for-an-early-neolithic-in-sub-saharan-africa/.

Iniguez, N. (2020, February 28). The Rise, Decline, and Collapse of the Aksum Empire. Retrieved from Storymaps.arcgis.com: https://storymaps.arcgis.com/stories/9b7b377398724be99a0d94dfa9f55550.

Jones, M. (2024, January 3). The Second Punic War (218-201 BC): Hannibal Marches Against Rome. Retrieved from Historyooperative.org: https://historycooperative.org/second-punic-war-hannibals-war-in-italy/.

K. Krois. Hirst. (2019, May 12). The Kingdom of Kush: Sub-Saharan African Rulers of the Nile. Retrieved from Thoughtco.com: https://www.thoughtco.com/the-kingdom-of-kush-171464.

Kemezis, K. (2009, November 22). Ancient Kush (2nd Millennium B.C. - 4th Century A.D.). Retrieved from Blackpast.org: https://www.blackpast.org/global-african-history/ancient-kush-2nd-millennium-b-c-4th-century-d/.

Kessing, F. M. (2024, January 9). Stone Age-African Tools, Artifacts, Culture. Retrieved from Britannca.com: https://www.britannica.com/event/Stone-Age/Africa.

King, A. (2018, July 25). The Economy of Ptolemaic Egypt. Retrieved from Worldhistory.org: https://www.worldhistory.org/article/1256/the-economy-of-ptolemaic-egypt/.

Kipling, Rudyard (1899). The White Man's Burden. https://historymatters.gmu.edu/d/5478/.

Koutonin, M. (2016, August 18). Lost Cities: Racism and Ruins—The Plundering of Great Zimbabwe. Retrieved from Theguardian.com: https://www.theguardian.com/cities/2016/aug/18/great-zimbabwe-medieval-lost-city-racism-ruins-plundering.

Lane, M. (2024, January 21). How Did Muslims and Non-Muslims Interact in Ghana. Retrieved from Ncesc.com: https://www.ncesc.com/geographic-faq/how-did-muslims-and-non-muslims-interact-in-ghana/

LibreTexts. (2024, January 27). 12.6 The Ghana Empire. Retrieved from LibreTexts.org: https://human.libretexts.org/Courses/Lumen_Learning/Book%3A_Early_World_Civilizations_(Lumen)/Ch._11_African_Civilizations/12.6%3A_The_Ghana_Empire#:~:text=Ghana%E2%80%99s%20economic%20development%20and%20eventual%20wealth%20was%20linked,expansion%20to%20.

LibreTexts. (2024, January 22). 4.2 Ancient Carthage. Retrieved from Libretexts.org: https://human.libretexts.org/Courses/Lumen_Learning/Book%3A_Early_World_Civilizations_(Lumen)/Ch._03_Early_Civilizations_of_Africa_and_the_Andes/04.2%3A_Ancient_Carthage.

Lifepersona.com. (2024, January 19). The 9 Most Important Contributions of Egypt to Humanity. Retrieved from Lifepersona.com: https://www.lifepersona.com/the-9-most-important-contributions-of-egypt-to-humanity.

Lynch, P. (201, May 5). A Brutal and Bloody Affair: 6 Key Battles That Decided the First Punic War. Retrieved from Historycollection.com: https://historycollection.com/roman-military-might-6-key-battles-decided-first-punic-war/.

Marc. (2022, October 14). The Kush Kingdom: A Major Power in the Ancient World. Retrieved from Ilovelanguages.com: https://www.ilovelanguages.com/the-kush-kingdom-a-major-power-in-the-ancient-world/.

Mark, J. J. (2016, November 9). Ancient Egyptian Science & Technology. Retrieved from World History Encyclopedia: https://www.worldhistory.org/article/967/ancient-egyptian-science--technology/.

Mark, J. J. (2017, September 21). Social Structure in Ancient Egypt. Retrieved from History World Encyclopedia: https://www.worldhistory.org/article/1123/social-structure-in-ancient-egypt/.

Mark, J. J. (2023, July 25). Library of Alexandria. Retrieved from Worldhistory.org: https://www.worldhistory.org/Library_of_Alexandria/.

Mummified Baboons Point to the Direction of the Fabled Land of Punt. (2023, November 11). Retrieved from Ars Technica: https://arstechnica.com/science/2023/11/mummified-baboons-point-to-the-direction-of-the-fabled-land-of-punt/.

Museum, T. B. (2024, January 9). Rock art and the origins of art in Africa. Retrieved from Khanacademy.org:

https://www.khanacademy.org/humanities/ap-art-history/global-prehistory-ap/paleolithic-mesolithic-neolithic-apah/a/apollo-11-stones.

New World Encyclopedia. (2024, January 19). Ptolemaic Dynasty. Retrieved from New World Encyclopedia: https://www.newworldencyclopedia.org/entry/Ptolemaic_dynasty.

New World Encyclopedia. (2024, January 25). Aksumite Empire. Retrieved from NewWorldEncuclopedia.org: https://www.newworldencyclopedia.org/entry/Aksumite_Empire.

New World Encyclopedia. (2024, January 27). Ghana Empire. Retrieved from New World Encyclopedia: https://www.newworldencyclopedia.org/entry/Ghana_Empire.

Openstax.org. (2024, January 13). 9.2 The Emergence of Farming and the Bantu Migrations. Retrieved from Openstax.org: https://openstax.org/books/world-history-volume-1/pages/9-2-the-emergence-of-farming-and-the-bantu-migrations.

Pbs.org. (2024, January 19). Art & Architecture. Retrieved from Pbs.org: https://www.pbs.org/empires/egypt/newkingdom/architecture.html.

Peter F. Dorman, M. S. (2024, January 19). Thutmose III. Retrieved from Britannica.com: https://www.britannica.com/biography/Thutmose-III/Adornment-of-Egypt.

Pressbooks.bccampus.ca. (2024, January 19). Middle Kingdom Art. Retrieved from Art and Visual Culture: Prehistory to Renaissance: https://pressbooks.bccampus.ca/cavestocathedrals/chapter/middle-kingdom/.

Pressbooks.bccampus.ca. (2024, January 19). New Kingdom Art. Retrieved from pressbooks.bccampus.ca: https://pressbooks.bccampus.ca/cavestocathedrals/chapter/new-kingdom/.

Robert Maddin, T. S. (1977). Tin in the Ancient Near East: Old Questions and New Finds. Retrieved from Penn Museum: https://www.penn.museum/sites/expedition/tin-in-the-ancient-near-east/.

Ross, E. G. (2002, October). The Age of Iron in West Africa. Retrieved from Metmuseum.org: https://www.metmuseum.org/toah/hd/iron/hd_iron.htm.

S., A. (2015, December 21). Mesolithic Social Life and Art. Retrieved from Shorthistory.org: https://www.shorthistory.org/prehistory/mesolithic-social-life-and-art/.

Scoville, P. (2015, November 6). Amarna Letters. Retrieved from Worldhistory.org: https://www.worldhistory.org/Amarna_Letters/.

Shuttleworth, M. (2024, January 28). Egyptian Astronomy. Retrieved from Explorable.com: https://explorable.com/egyptian-astronomy.

Smith, P. (2015, September 16). Nabta Playa: The Oldest Man-Made Structure in the World. Retrieved from Historic Cornwell: https://www.historic-cornwall.org.uk/nabta-playa-the-oldest-man-made-structure-in-the-world/.

Smithsonian Institute. (2024, January 3). Climate Effects on Human Evolution. Retrieved from Humanorigons.si.edu: https://humanorigins.si.edu/research/climate-and-human-evolution/climate-effects-human-evolution.

Soto, N. (2024, January 16). Who Destroyed the Ghana Empire. Retrieved from Ncesc.com: https://www.ncesc.com/geographic-faq/who-destroyed-the-ghana-empire/.

Staff, E. (2021, October 31). Carthaginian Trade: Trade Routes of Ancient Carthage. Retrieved from Carthagemagazine.com: https://carthagemagazine.com/carthaginian-trade-routes-of-ancient-carthage/.

Taronas, L. (2024, January 19). Akhenaten: The Mysteries of Religious Revolution. Retrieved from Arce.org: https://arce.org/resource/akhenaten-mysteries-religious-revolution/.

Team, E. (2018, October 21). Kingdom of Punt: When Ancient Egypt Envied Somalia. Retrieved from Thinkafrica.net: https://thinkafrica.net/land-of-punt/.

Team, E. (2018, November 3). The Kingdom of Kerma (2500-1500 BC). Retrieved from Thinkafrica.net: https://thinkafrica.net/the-kingdom-of-kerma-2500-1500-bc/.

Thomas Garnet, H. J. (2024, January 13). Egyptian Art and Architecture. Retrieved from Britannca.com: https://www.britannica.com/topic/Martin-Luther-King-Jr-1929-68-2229053

Tyson, P. (2009, December 1). Where is Punt? Retrieved from PBS.org: https://www.pbs.org/wgbh/nova/article/egypt-punt/.

Wasson, D. L. (2016, September 29). Ptolemaic Dynasty. Retrieved from Worldhistory.org: https://www.worldhistory.org/Ptolemaic_Dynasty/.

Wendorg, M. (2023, April 23). Ancient Egyptian Technology and Inventions. Retrieved from Interesting Enginerring.com: https://interestingengineering.com/lists/ancient-egyptian-technology-and-inventions.